Thank You
♥ OPERATION
BBQ RELIEF
YOU GUYS ARE AWESOME

GRILLING

with **Golic** and **Hays**

Dedicated to all the volunteers, supporters, and sponsors of Operation BBQ Relief

GRILLING

with **Golic** and **Hays**

 **OPERATION BBQ RELIEF** Cookbook

MIKE GOLIC and STAN HAYS

Photography by Ken Goodman

Andrews McMeel
PUBLISHING®

CONTENTS

Chapter 6
BURGERS and SANDWICHES . . . 95

Chapter 7
SEAFOOD . . . 111

Chapter 8
DESSERTS . . . 131

Chapter 9
DRINKS . . . 143

Chapter 10
RUBS and SAUCES . . . 157

Introduction

THE HEALING POWER OF BBQ

Armed with a caravan of cooks, mobile pits, kitchens, and volunteers, Operation BBQ Relief delivers the healing power of barbecue in times of need, feeding first responders and communities affected by natural disasters along with year-round efforts to fight hunger through The Always Serving Project® and Operation Restaurant Relief™.

Operation BBQ Relief, a 501(c)(3) nonprofit, was founded in May 2011 in response to a need for tornado relief efforts in Joplin, Missouri. Competitive pitmasters and grillmasters from eight states answered the call to feed displaced families and first responders. Together, they served more than 120,000 meals in a 13-day period. Little did they know, 10 years later, that a hundred volunteers would turn into thousands, 120,000 meals would turn into millions, and this one act of love would turn into a movement that spread across the nation.

The mission of Operation BBQ Relief continues as natural disasters, including floods, hurricanes, tornadoes, and fires, disrupt and destroy communities. Operation BBQ Relief closely monitors impending natural disasters throughout the United States, staging and deploying assets to serve as soon as possible, usually within 24–48 hours.

"Our teams and volunteers work around the clock to ensure communities in need receive a hot meal, letting those affected by natural disasters know that they are not forgotten," said Stan Hays, CEO and cofounder. "If you just lost your home, a hot meal can provide comfort and some immediate relief in the wake of devastation."

Since 2011, Operation BBQ Relief has been deployed 84 times, serving more than 9 million meals in 30 US states as well as one international deployment to the Bahamas. Like many communities in the past decade, Operation BBQ Relief has been through a lot. Staff and volunteers have responded to disasters nationwide, from Hurricane Superstorm Sandy in 2012, to Hurricane Harvey in 2017, to Hurricane Michael in 2018, to Hurricane Dorian in 2019, as well as wildfires, tornadoes, derechos—and a pandemic that upturned a nation in 2020. Together in these moments of crisis, Operation BBQ Relief has rallied together, rebuilding hope and accomplishing many feats.

HOUSTON, TEXAS—HURRICANE HARVEY
(August 2017): 371,760 meals served over 11 days

Hurricane Harvey, a Category 4 hurricane, struck Texas and neighboring states after making landfall on August 17, 2017. Hurricane Harvey caused catastrophic flooding and an estimated $125 billion in damages. Operation BBQ Relief was personally invited by Mayor of Houston, Sylvester Turner, to feed first responders and city workers.

With the help of the Houston Police Helicopter Department and the National Guard, Operation BBQ Relief airlifted meals from Houston Hobby Airport to the Beaumont, Texas, Convention Center in Beaumont, Texas. This was the first airlift Operation BBQ Relief had ever done. As Operation BBQ Relief fed the community, the organization received media attention like never before on national television. Part of the CNN Heroes Documentary was filmed during this deployment, as CEO and co-founder Stan Hays was recognized for his work as a CNN Hero. Fox News also shot a one-hour show from the deployment site.

This deployment quickly became the largest disaster Operation BBQ Relief had responded to—it was the largest in meal total, number of volunteers engaged, and amount of donations received. Operation BBQ Relief hit another milestone by serving 55,000 hot meals that mattered in one day alone to the Houston community. This deployment showed that Operation BBQ Relief was ready to serve, no matter how large the disaster. Over 371,000 meals were served in Houston during the 11-day deployment.

NAPA/SANTA ROSA, CALIFORNIA—WILDFIRES

(October 2017): 53,058 meals served over 8 days

In October 2017, Operation BBQ Relief was invited to deploy to its very first wildfire disaster in Napa and Santa Rosa, California. Generally, the thought of bringing smoke and fire to a wildfire is not one that most emergency managers want to talk about. Even with Operation BBQ Relief's safety methods, the idea of barbecue is not always thought of during disasters like these.

Thankfully, this community welcomed Operation BBQ Relief to serve those most in need. The request to help the community came from well-known Food Network star Guy Fieri. His home was evacuated, and he wanted to ensure that his community was helped.

Operation BBQ Relief was honored to share the healing power of barbecue alongside celebrity chefs. This deployment created a network of Operation BBQ Relief volunteers from coast to coast. By increasing equipment, volunteers, and resources west of the Rocky Mountains, Operation BBQ Relief became equipped to help during any natural disaster nationwide.

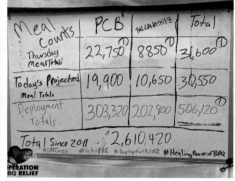

Meal Counts	PCB	TALLAHASSEE	Total
Thursday Meal Totals	22,750	8850	31,600
Today's Projected Meal Totals	19,900	10,650	30,550
Deployment Totals	303,320	202,800	506,120
Total Since 2011		2,610,420	

#OBRCares #UchtOBR #DeployedwithOBR #HealingPowerofBBQ

OPERATION BQ RELIEF

TALLAHASSEE/PANAMA CITY, FLORIDA—HURRICANE MICHAEL
(October 2018): 808,220 meals served over 30 days

After Hurricane Michael in Florida, Operation BBQ Relief set up one of their longest-running deployments to serve that one hot meal that matters. This deployment lasted 30 days: 30 days of volunteers dedicating their time, 30 days of meals served, 30 days of sharing the healing power of barbecue.

This also was the first major deployment to have two primary volunteer sites running independently of each other. The first site was run like a traditional deployment, while the second included an onsite RV park for their volunteers to bring their own trailers. The two sites helped cover the panhandle of Florida with meals and sent meals to affected communities in Georgia. Operation BBQ Relief volunteers shared their time for almost an entire month to serve communities in need.

GRAND BAHAMA ISLAND—HURRICANE DORIAN
(September 2019): 88,515 meals served over 15 days

Operation BBQ Relief's first international deployment occurred in September 2019 when volunteers traveled to Grand Bahama Island to serve meals to the residents affected by Hurricane Dorian. Hurricane Dorian inflicted catastrophic damage in the Bahamas as the hurricane came to a complete standstill over the northwest Bahamian islands for more than 24 hours. Operation BBQ Relief coordinated with emergency management agencies to determine where efforts were most needed. They determined that Grand Bahama Island was in desperate need of Operation BBQ Relief's support.

To complete this deployment successfully, Operation BBQ Relief had two teams of volunteers. One team remained in Florida, and another traveled to the Bahamas.

All the meals were produced in Florida, then airlifted by plane daily to the island by the WWII-era C-47 plane *Miss Montana*. The team on the island then transported the food to a local church that was one of the hubs for services and handed out the meals each evening.

Flying meals to their destination brought an additional dimension of logistical complexity to the normal deployment activities. Inclement weather, airplane mechanical issues, and Freeport airport closings all impacted meal delivery unexpectedly. This teamwork of volunteers, sponsors, local businesses, and churches in both Ft. Lauderdale and Freeport allowed Operation BBQ Relief's first international deployment to be incredibly successful.

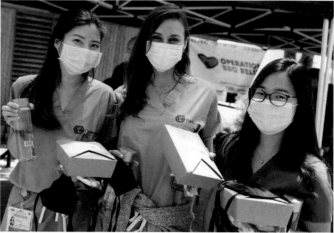
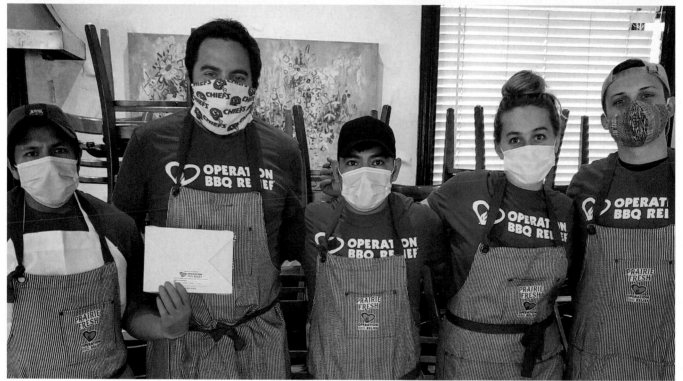

COVID-19 PANDEMIC

(March 2020): Over 5 million meals served throughout the year

The year 2020 was full of challenges for many. The uncertainty of living through a pandemic weighed on many people. The COVID-19 pandemic also created an opportunity for Operation BBQ Relief to step up and help.

It turned out that 2020 was the biggest year for Operation BBQ Relief yet. Over 5 million meals were served, and 4 million of those meals were served to people directly impacted by COVID-19.

WINTER STORM—HOUSTON, TEXAS
(February 2021): 37,000 meals served over 9 days

Operation BBQ Relief provided 37,000 hot barbecue meals in response to Winter Storm Uri in Houston. The historic winter storm broke pipes and left hundreds of thousands of residents without power and water access. Meals were delivered to seniors and individuals with disabilities. Operation BBQ Relief celebrated the nine-millionth meal with Mayor Sylvester Turner during a drive-through pickup distribution in Houston.

Operation BBQ Relief has deployed to areas devastated by hurricanes, tornadoes, and derechos to serve that one hot meal that matters. In addition to traditional deployments, Operation BBQ Relief started a new initiative called Operation Restaurant Relief™.

This program allowed restaurants and caterers to remain open or helped them to reopen despite the nationwide lockdowns on dining. It allowed restaurant businesses to keep their lights on and their employees paid, all while serving their community. Operation BBQ Relief found new ways of helping people during a pandemic and provided solutions to many different organizations and communities.

As of 2021, Operation BBQ Relief has reached a milestone of over 9 million meals. That's over 9 million hearts touched in the span of our movement, over 9 million moments of sharing the healing power of barbecue.

HAMMOND, LOUISIANA—HURRICANE IDA
(August 2021): 247,055 meals served over 21 days

After Hurricane Ida made landfall with 150 mph winds as a Category 4 hurricane, Operation BBQ Relief arrived to work around the clock to ensure families, first responders, utility workers, front-line essential employees, and communities received a comforting hot meal. Operation BBQ Relief connects with communities by providing hope, compassion, and friendship to those in need of meals as the recovery efforts continue. The damage was significant with over 1 million households without water or power.

Operation BBQ Relief helped airlift meals to hard hit areas like Houma, delivered meals to New Orleans, and provided drive-thru lunch and dinner services for families in Hammond, Louisiana.

They met many families who were deeply grateful during the drive-thru distribution. Barbara picked up meals with her two young boys and neighbors. She said her neighbor was dying with cancer and they hated each other for years over petty little things. When she shared the meals from Operation BBQ Relief with her neighbor, they cried and made amends. They hugged for the first time in years as she said her neighbor hadn't eaten in days and that single act of kindness of sharing the one hot meal that matters made all the negativity go away. This story is one of the millions that highlight the powerful impact of the healing power BBQ.

Operation BBQ Relief has deployed to Louisiana several times over the years. In 2016 they served their one millionth meal in Hammond, and in 2020 they provided over 400,000 meals following Hurricanes Laura and Delta to Louisiana residents.

TIPS

for Grilling and Smoking

1. **Buy a meat thermometer.** Even experienced cooks use thermometers, because it is difficult to know whether meat is done just by looking at it or touching it. By using a meat thermometer, you know the exact temperature.

2. **Keep a spray bottle handy for flare-ups.** Too many flames can cause a lot of char, which can be unpleasant to eat. Have a spray bottle filled with water handy to spray flare-ups as needed.

3. **Don't cook to the internal temperature wanted.** When you remove the meat from the grill, it continues to cook. Removing it before it hits your desired temperature will allow it to continue cooking and reach your desired temperature. If you leave meat on the grill until it reaches the desired temperature, you run the risk of overcooking it.

4. **Don't flatten your meat while on the grill.** When you take that spatula and squish your burger, you are pushing fatty juices into the grill. This can cause flare-ups, and your meat will lose its juicy flavor.

5. **Keep your grill and smoker clean.** You don't want pieces of meat from last night's dinner mixing with tonight's dinner. Some meats, like chicken, pick up unwanted flavor from unclean grills and leave an unwanted taste.

6. **Rest your meat after smoking.** The longer your meat stays on the grill, the more energy or heat it absorbs. This causes all the juicy flavor to be pushed to the surface. If you remove your meat and cut it right away, all the juicy flavor leaks out. If you let it rest first, the heat and juice will redistribute throughout the meat and leave a more delicious flavor.

7. **If you want deep, rich flavor, make sure to marinate or inject your meats.** Marinating and injecting get flavors inside your meat. They will help tenderize and keep your meat moist.

8. **Start with the best meat.** You want to start with good, high-quality meat. For example, when cooking beef, you want it to be well marbled and have a good color to it. This will lead to consistently great results each time.

9. **If you're looking, you ain't cooking.** If you keep opening the lid and checking the temperature of your meat, you cannot keep a consistent temperature inside your pit. These fluctuations in temperature will cause inconsistencies in your cooking. Remember: low and slow cooking means be patient! Check your temperature on long cooks only every hour as you get close to finishing.

10. **Air circulation is key.** When barbecuing, you want to make sure that the pieces of meat are not touching each other. The meat will take longer to cook, and each piece of meat's internal temperature will not be consistent. Make sure to buy a large enough grill or smoker based on what you plan to cook.

OPERATION BBQ RELIEF SEASONINGS MENTIONED THROUGHOUT THE BOOK

Operation BBQ Relief Sweet & Smoky Rub: a brown sugar and hickory smoke blend. Best on beef, poultry, and fish. Inspired by Joplin, Missouri, tornado disaster relief response in 2011.

In 2011, an EF-5 tornado destroyed the town of Joplin, Missouri. From that destruction, came Operation BBQ Relief. The morning after the tornado, phone calls were made between old friends who knew they needed to do something to help the community. By mid-day, a Facebook page was created. The all-call was put out to the BBQ community and anyone else who wanted to come help. Less than 48 hours after that phone call, barbecue pits, food, and volunteers were on the ground in Joplin, Missouri. The very first hot meals made it into the hands of people who needed it most. It was very apparent that a gap existed between when natural disasters strike and when those communities can be helped. Operation BBQ Relief was created to fill that gap. Who better to fill this gap than a bunch of barbecue enthusiasts who set up in parking lots to compete against each other? Only this time, their skills as pitmasters were going to be used to come together and cook barbecue for communities in need and first responders. At the beginning, volunteers thought they would be in Joplin for three or four days and only serve about 5,000 meals. After 11 days, Operation BBQ Relief served over 120,000 meals to first responders and families affected by the tornado.

Operation BBQ Relief All-Purpose Rub: a well-balanced blend of garlic, herbs, and spices. Best on beef, pork, poultry, fish, and vegetables. Inspired by Moore, Oklahoma, tornado relief efforts in 2012.

The town of Moore, Oklahoma, knows the effects of natural disasters a little too well. This town has been hit by over 23 tornadoes, and its citizens know the devastation that occurs after them. In May of 2013, the town of Moore faced yet another deadly tornado. The very next day, Operation BBQ Relief was serving meals to first responders and working to get the deployment site set up. For Stan Hays, CEO and co-founder, one of the hardest things for him was going to the Plaza Towers Elementary to take food and check on the crew that was serving in that neighborhood. When he pulled up to the school, he pulled up next to the fence that had the homemade crosses for the kids who lost their lives in the tornado. The reality of what happened and the hurt the community felt was seen that day. Many times, we don't see it up close and personal, but Stan saw the notes written on those crosses and the love that the community showed for those children. Several years later, he still gets emotional in communities when he sees memorials like this. He will never forget the site at Plaza Towers Elementary that day.

Operation BBQ Relief Cajun Bayou Rub: a spicy and traditional Louisiana blend. Best on beef, pork, seafood, and vegetables. Inspired by Louisiana flooding, 2016.

Operation BBQ Relief was deployed to Hammond, Louisiana, after 25 inches of rain caused massive flooding in the community. The volunteers set up in a high, dry area at a closed-down school that happened to still have a power supply. Hammond was a big deployment for Operation BBQ Relief. This became one of the largest deployments in numbers and geographic size at the time. The volunteers were running food over 100 miles one way to a drop-off point. That food was then taken another 100 miles to feeding locations. Operation BBQ Relief served its one millionth meal during this deployment and gained lifelong friendships and volunteers along the way. 312,587 meals were served in Hammond over 13 days.

Operation BBQ Relief Texas SPG Rub: a traditional Texas salt, pepper, and garlic blend. Best on beef, pork, poultry, fish, and vegetables. Inspired by Hurricane Harvey relief efforts in 2017.

Following Hurricane Harvey, Operation BBQ Relief served 371,760 meals and established many lifelong friendships in the city of Houston. The deployment in Houston was a nationally recognized relief effort. Multiple news outlets throughout the country covered the relief work by Operation BBQ Relief. The mayor of Houston, Sylvester Turner, personally invited Operation BBQ Relief to feed first responders and city workers.

This was the first airlift Operation BBQ Relief had ever done. With the help of the Houston Police Helicopter Department and the National Guard, Operation BBQ Relief airlifted meals from Houston Hobby Airport to the Convention Center in Beaumont, Texas.

Operation BBQ Relief Florida Mojo Rub: a Cuban blend of garlic, citrus, and cumin. Best on fish, poultry, pork, and vegetables. Inspired by relief efforts after Hurricane Irma in 2017 and Hurricane Michael in 2018.

Hurricane Irma was classified as a Category 4 hurricane when it made landfall in Florida on Sept. 10, 2017. Although downgraded over time, Irma caused widespread damage via storm surges, high winds, and rainfall, causing power loss, flooding, and major damage. Operation BBQ Relief deployed to Southwest Florida and spent 9 days, serving 126,400 meals. In addition, FedEx assisted by flying meals to the Florida Keys.

After Hurricane Michael in Florida, Operation BBQ Relief set up one of their longest running deployments to serve that one hot meal that matters. This deployment lasted 30 days. 30 days of volunteers dedicating their time. 30 days of meals served. 30 days of sharing the healing power of barbecue. This also was the first major deployment to have two primary volunteer sites running independently of each other. The first site was run like a traditional deployment while the second included an onsite RV park for their volunteers to bring their own trailers. The two sites helped cover the panhandle of Florida with meals as well as sent meals to affected communities in Georgia. Operation BBQ Relief volunteers shared their time for almost an entire month to serve over 808,000 meals.

Operation BBQ Relief Santa Maria Steak Rub: a California blend of smoked paprika, garlic, and spices. Best on beef, pork, poultry, and vegetables. Inspired by catastrophic wildfires that devastated California in 2019.

Seasonal winds fanned the flames of wildfires across California vegetation dried out due to delayed fall rains. The Kincade Fire was the largest of the 2019 California wildfires, burning over 77,000 acres. When mandatory evacuations around Sonoma County, California, were put in place, Operation BBQ Relief was asked to come help feed those impacted. We immediately deployed a local team to Petaluma, California, where we fed 200 hot meals to impacted residents in shelters and first responders. Within 24 hours, firefighters were able to improve containment enough that the Sonoma County Sheriff's Office lifted some and downgraded other evacuation orders in connection with the Kincade Fire, allowing residents to go back to their homes. This deployment was a great reminder that regardless of the number of days deployed or the total number of meals provided, it is all about providing the one hot meal that matters.

Chapter 1
APPETIZERS

BRISKET-STUFFED JALAPEÑOS
JOHNNY IMBRIOLO

Jalapeños are the perfect bite-size appetizer. Stuff these peppers with brisket and now you have a hearty and flavorful bite. These jalapeños are full of big, bold flavors inspired by the spicy and smoky flavors of the Lone Star State of Texas.

15 pickled whole jalapeños

STUFFING
7 ounces smoked brisket, coarsely chopped

2 tablespoons homemade barbecue sauce

½ ounce chipotle peppers in adobo sauce, chopped

1 tablespoon apple cider vinegar

1 tablespoon ketchup

3 ounces shredded pepper jack cheese

½ cup all-purpose flour

2 large eggs, beaten

½ cup panko bread crumbs

½ cup ranch dressing, for serving

Drain the jalapeños from their juice. Cut each in half lengthwise, leaving the stem connected. Leave about ¼ inch at the stem to ensure that the jalapeño stays intact when stuffed. Using a small spoon, carefully scrape out the seeds.

To make the stuffing, place the brisket, barbecue sauce, chipotle peppers, vinegar, ketchup, and cheese in a large bowl and mix well.

Place 1 tablespoon stuffing inside each jalapeño, keeping the natural shape of the pepper. Repeat with the remaining jalapeños and stuffing.

Place the flour, eggs, and panko bread crumbs in separate small dishes.

First, coat the stuffed jalapeño in flour, then in egg, and, finally, in bread crumbs. Make sure the jalapeño is completely coated with bread crumbs, then place it on a large, flat dish and repeat with the remaining jalapeños.

Prepare a deep fryer to 350°F. Carefully place five of the stuffed jalapeños at a time in the fryer. Cook for 3 to 4 minutes, until the internal temperature reaches 140°F and the jalapeños are golden brown. Carefully remove them with a slotted spoon and place them on a plate lined with paper towels to drain. Repeat with the remaining jalapeños. Serve them while still warm with a side of ranch dressing.

YIELD: 5 servings

SMOKED JALAPEÑO PIMENTO CHEESE

STAN HAYS

Easy to assemble but still delicious! This dip by Operation BBQ Relief's CEO Stan Hays is an excellent choice to share at any party because it combines the smoky flavors of jalapeños as well as sweeter notes of pimentos. It can be quickly made ahead of time and stored in the refrigerator until ready to serve.

2 (8-ounce) blocks cream cheese

3 jalapeños

1 (2-ounce) jar diced pimientos

¾ cup real mayonnaise

1½ tablespoons Weber Roasted Garlic and Herb Seasoning or your favorite spice blend

8 ounces shredded cheddar cheese

8 ounces shredded pepper jack cheese

Salt and freshly ground black pepper

Chips or crackers, for serving

Prepare a grill to 200°F. Place the cream cheese in a small heatproof dish and smoke for 45 minutes to 1 hour, until golden brown.

Place the jalapeños on the grill grate and smoke for about 20 minutes, or until golden brown. Rotate them after 10 minutes.

Once the jalapeños are smoked, remove them from the grill and let them cool slightly. Coarsely dice them and place them in a medium bowl. Drain the pimientos.

Add the cream cheese and pimientos to the bowl with the jalapeños, along with the remaining ingredients. Mix well to combine. Cover and refrigerate overnight to let the flavors blend.

Serve with your favorite chips or crackers.

YIELD: 8 to 10 servings

© James Edward Bates

SMOKED CREAM CHEESE

STAN HAYS

Kick up any recipe that includes cream cheese by substituting this smoked cream cheese. It is also delicious when chilled in a log with salsa over the top with tortilla chips or with a spicy jelly over the top with crackers.

1 (8-ounce) block cream cheese

Place a block of cream cheese, in all its packaging, in the freezer for an hour before placing it in the smoker.

Start your smoker, making a small fire with your favorite wood; cherrywood or applewood works best. Try to keep the temperature low, around 150°F or below, so the cream cheese has a chance to take on the smoke and doesn't just melt. The smoking process can even be repeated for a smokier flavor. If the cream cheese is too hot and melts, it may need to be placed in the refrigerator to reharden.

Unwrap the cream cheese and place it in a small foil pan without a cover. Place the pan away from the fire on the coolest spot of the smoker.

Smoke it for 45 minutes to 1 hour, depending on the temperature of the smoker. The outside of the cream cheese should turn golden brown. Remove the pan from the smoker.

While still warm, mix the cream cheese together thoroughly. It is best to let it cool overnight, to allow the flavor to bloom throughout before using. But if it's needed right away, it will still be great. Enjoy it by itself on crackers or mixed in with dips.

YIELD: 6 servings

SOUTHWEST SHRIMP COCKTAIL

MIKE GOLIC

This recipe is a Southwest twist on a classic appetizer. Tender shrimp, zesty lemon, avocado, and pico de gallo combine to make this dish unforgettable. This recipe is easily multiplied for a crowd.

3 ounces diced cooked shrimp

3 tablespoons salsa

3 tablespoons Bloody Mary mix

1 tablespoon chopped fresh cilantro

½ avocado, pitted, peeled, and diced

½ cup pico de gallo

3 fresh cilantro leaves, for garnish

⅔ fresh lime, for garnish

4 tortilla chips, for serving

Place the shrimp, salsa, Bloody Mary mix, cilantro, avocado, and pico de gallo in a small bowl and mix until well combined.

Place the mixture in a large margarita glass. Garnish with the cilantro leaves and lime. Serve with the tortilla chips.

YIELD: 1 serving

SMOKED DEVILED EGGS
MIKE GOLIC JR.

A smoky take on a classic appetizer! With only a few minutes on your grill, your deviled eggs will reach the next level, making them perfect for any backyard barbecue or tailgate.

6 large eggs

2 slices bacon

¼ cup real mayonnaise

1 teaspoon white vinegar

1 teaspoon Carolina mustard sauce or your favorite mustard sauce

Salt and freshly ground black pepper

Pinch of smoked paprika

Place the eggs in a medium saucepan, covering completely with water, over high heat. When the water starts boiling, turn the heat to low and cover the pan for 1 minute. Turn the heat off, move the pan from the burner and let sit for 15 minutes.

While the eggs are resting, cook the strips of bacon in a frying pan over medium heat until crisp. Remove the bacon from the pan to a plate lined with paper towels to drain.

Drain the water from the eggs. Crack the eggs and peel the shells while rinsing under cold water.

Start a smoker using a fruit wood, such as apple or cherry, and heat it to 250°F. Place the eggs straight onto the smoker grate and cook them for 10 minutes.

Remove the eggs from the smoker and slice them in half, removing the yolks to a medium bowl. Mash the yolks with a fork so they are in crumbles. Add the mayonnaise, vinegar, mustard sauce, and salt and pepper. Mix well until smooth.

Use a small spoon to place a rounded teaspoon of the mixture in each egg white. Sprinkle paprika over the top of each.

Crack each strip of bacon into several 2-inch pieces. Place a piece on top of each egg half and serve.

YIELD: 6 servings

MARINATED GRILLED VEGETABLE CRUDITÉ

JUSTIN REED

Cooking for numerous VIP events and feeding the masses for the Coast Guard, Justin Reed stepped up the crudité platter and started grilling and marinating vegetables with balsamic marinade. Guests will love it, and like barbeque foods, it is irresistible. These are best eaten the same day and do not reheat well.

MARINADE

2 cups balsamic vinegar (use aged balsamic for a more intense flavor)

1 cup olive oil

1 cup warm water

¼ cup chopped garlic

2 tablespoons Montreal steak seasoning or your favorite seasoning

2 Vidalia onions, cut into ½-inch slices, similar to onion rings

8 ounces cremini or button mushrooms, whole

1 zucchini, quartered lengthwise and cut into 1-inch pieces

1 yellow squash, quartered lengthwise and cut into 1-inch pieces

1 pound asparagus, 1½ inches trimmed from the bottom

2 medium-sized red peppers, seeded and cut into 1½-inch strips

1 cup crumbled feta cheese

To make the marinade, place all the ingredients in a large bowl and whisk to combine. Set aside.

Wash and dry the vegetables, then prepare as directed. Place the cut vegetables in their own 1-gallon resealable plastic bags: there should be one bag of zucchini, one bag of yellow squash, one bag of asparagus, one bag of mushrooms, one bag of onions, and one bag of peppers. Divide the marinade evenly between the six plastic bags, ensuring there is enough marinade in each bag to coat and soak each vegetable. For a more intense flavor, splash the contents of each bag with additional balsamic vinegar before sealing the bag. Be sure to close each bag tightly to minimize the amount of air. Place the bags in the refrigerator and marinate overnight.

Remove the vegetables from each plastic bag, reserving the marinade. Place the vegetables in a shallow dish to transport to the grill, keeping the vegetables in separate groups.

Preheat a grill to 350°F. Grill each vegetable for about 5 minutes and turn them while cooking. When you start to see grill marks, they are ready to come off.

Place the vegetables back in their shallow dishes and pour any remaining marinade back on top.

Place the vegetables on a platter in separate groups, showcasing the grill marks. Again, pour the remaining marinade from the shallow dish over the vegetables.

Sprinkle the feta over the top and serve at room temperature.

YIELD: 8 servings

GRILLED AVOCADO GUACAMOLE

BEN BRAUNECKER

Freshly made guacamole should be a staple at any house party. This recipe calls for the avocado pieces to be grilled first. With char marks added to the avocado, the guacamole takes on a smoky flavor that can be added only by using the grill!

4 avocados

1 jalapeño, halved lengthwise and seeded

2 tablespoons canola oil

¼ teaspoon kosher salt

¼ cup minced red onion

2 large cloves garlic, minced

1 fresh Roma tomato, diced

2 tablespoons coarsely chopped fresh cilantro

½ teaspoon Operation BBQ Relief Florida Mojo Rub or your favorite rub

½ fresh lime

Tortilla chips, for serving

Cut the avocados in half and remove the pits. Peel off the outer skin and place the avocados, cut side up, on a large sheet pan. Place the jalapeño on the tray with the avocado. Drizzle the oil over the avocado and jalapeño, then season with salt.

Preheat a grill to 350°F. Place the avocado and jalapeño, cut side down, on the grill. Grill for 30 seconds, then rotate 180°F and grill for 30 seconds more, to create a cross grill mark. Flip the avocado and jalapeño over and grill for 30 seconds more. Remove them from the grill and let cool.

Dice the avocado into ½-inch pieces and add to a medium bowl. Mince the jalapeño and add to the avocado. Add the red onion, garlic, tomatoes, and cilantro and mash all the ingredients well.

Season with rub. Squeeze the lime over the mixture and stir well. Serve with tortilla chips.

YIELD: 6 servings

SMOKED SPINACH & ARTICHOKE DIP

MIKE GOLIC

This is a great smoky twist on a classic appetizer. While a traditional spinach-artichoke dip is made in the oven, take this dish out to your smoker! Leaving the dish in the smoker adds unique aromas to an already delicious meal. A great recipe that is sure to kick up your backyard barbeque!

1 pound fresh whole artichokes

2 teaspoons canola oil

1 teaspoon kosher salt

1 teaspoon Operation BBQ Relief Sweet & Smoky Rub or your favorite rub

1 (8-ounce) block cream cheese

16 ounces fresh spinach

¼ cup water

6 ounces shredded Gouda cheese

6 ounces shredded Monterey jack cheese

4 cloves garlic, minced

1 cup real mayonnaise

½ teaspoon red pepper flakes

½ teaspoon smoked paprika

1 (12-ounce) bag tortilla chips, for serving

Preheat a smoker to 225°F.

While the smoker is heating, cut the stem and tip off the artichokes. Peel back the outer leaves of the artichoke until pale yellow leaves are exposed. Cut the artichoke in half lengthwise and pull out the choke in the center. The choke has a red tip and is very tough. There are thin fibers on the base of the choke—both should be removed. Using a teaspoon, carefully insert the spoon under the red leaves and, grasping the choke with your thumb, pull the choke toward the base until it rips free. Continue until all red pieces and thin fibers are removed.

Coat the artichokes with oil and season with salt and rub.

Place the artichokes in the smoker and smoke for about 1 hour, or until tender.

After removing it from all its packaging, place the cream cheese on aluminum foil, then set it in the smoker, and cook it for about 30 minutes, or until it turns light brown.

Remove the cream cheese and the artichokes and allow them to cool.

Place the spinach in a large sauté pan and add the water. Heat to a boil while covered. Remove the pan from the heat and drain the water. Pat the spinach dry with a paper towel.

Place the cream cheese in a large bowl. Finely chop the artichokes and add them to the cream cheese. Finely chop the cooked spinach and add it to the bowl.

Add the Gouda, Monterey jack, garlic, mayonnaise, and red pepper flakes. Mix well.

Place the dip into a medium baking dish and spread out the mixture evenly.

Sprinkle the top of the dip with the smoked paprika and place it in the smoker for about 20 minutes, or until it is deep golden brown.

Remove the dip from the smoker and serve with your favorite tortilla chips.

YIELD: 4 servings

SMOKED BRISKET WONTONS

JOHNNY IMBRIOLO

An Asian twist on a delicious barbecue dish! By packaging the smoked brisket inside the wonton wrapper, these snacks become the ultimate handheld appetizer. You could even make these wontons a meal by serving them with some apple coleslaw and pickled red onions.

Canola oil, for frying

8 ounces smoked brisket, chopped

3 ounces shredded pepper jack cheese

1 tablespoon chopped fresh cilantro

½ teaspoon Operation BBQ Relief Sweet & Smoky Rub or your favorite rub

¼ teaspoon kosher salt

2 tablespoons your favorite barbecue sauce

12 wonton wrappers

¼ cup water

Place the oil in a large pot over medium heat. Make sure the oil is at least 2 inches deep to ensure the wontons will be completely covered when cooking. The oil should reach 350°F.

In a large bowl add the brisket, cheese, cilantro, rub, salt, and barbecue sauce. Mix well.

Place a wonton wrapper on a cutting board and coat the edges lightly with water. Place 1 ounce of filling in the center of the wonton in an oblong shape. Fold the wrapper over to form a triangle, making sure there is no air trapped with the filling.

Brush the ends of the wonton lightly with water and fold them over to connect to each other, leaving the point facing up.

Repeat filling the remaining wontons using the same method.

Carefully drop the wontons in the hot oil and fry for 1 to 2 minutes, until golden brown. Remove the wontons from the oil and drain well on a paper towel–lined plate. Drizzle with your favorite barbecue sauce and enjoy!

YIELD: 4 servings

BARBECUE RIB LOLLIPOPS
MARK COLLINS

Enjoy sweet and savory barbecue rib lollipops by two-time Super Bowl Champion Mark Collins. Barbecue rib lollipops are a fun and easy appetizer to serve at tailgates or at home while rooting for your favorite sports team.

1 rack St. Louis ribs
1 tablespoon Lawry's Seasoned Salt
1 (12-ounce) can Dr. Pepper
16 ounces barbecue sauce
¼ cup Amaretto

Trim the excess fat off of the ribs. Remove any ribs on the ends that are thin and skinny. Turn the rack of ribs over and remove the membrane on the back of the ribs.

Cut each rib off of the rack, maximizing the amount of meat on the bone. Using a boning knife, score the back of the bone to release the meat. Pull the meat from the bone, making sure to keep the meat attached at the base of the bone, at least 1 inch.

Using a meat mallet, pound the meat to ¼-inch thickness. Using a fork, tenderize the meat by poking a few holes in the meat. Season both sides of the meat with Lawry's.

Wrap the meat around the base of the bone to make the lollipop. Insert a toothpick to hold the meat in place. Place the lollipops in an aluminum pan and pour the Dr. Pepper around the outside of the lollipops. Cover and refrigerate overnight.

The following day, remove the lollipops from the pan and discard the liquid. Preheat a smoker to 225°F.

Place the lollipops in the smoker and cook for approximately 1 hour.

While the lollipops are cooking, mix the barbecue sauce and Amaretto together.

After 1 hour, place the lollipops in an aluminum pan, baste with the Amaretto barbecue sauce, and cover with aluminum foil. Cook for an additional 2 to 3 hours, or until the meat is tender.

Remove the lollipops from the smoker and finish on the grill, basting with more Amaretto barbecue sauce. When the sauce is set on the lollipops, remove from the grill. Serve immediately.

YIELD: 3 servings

TRASH CAN NACHOS
BRYAN MROCZKA

Who wants a plate of nachos when you could have a towering stack of them? When you remove the can from the piled-high nachos, the cheese drips and slides down the mountain of chips. This will be the hit of the party!

1 (26-ounce) bag tortilla chips

2 pounds shredded cheddar cheese

2 pounds pulled pork

4 ounces sliced jalapeños (about 2 large jalapeños)

4 ounces diced Roma tomatoes

8 ounces white queso cheese dip

¼ cup sliced green onions, for garnish

Preheat a grill to 300°F.

Cut the bottom off an empty 109-ounce #10 standard size can and place the bottom on a medium cast-iron skillet.

Cover the bottom of the can with a layer of chips.

Sprinkle cheese over the chips. Layer the pulled pork over the cheese, then follow with the jalapenos over the pork. Finish with the tomatoes on top of the jalapenos.

Repeat with additional layers of chips, cheese, pulled pork, jalapeño, and tomato until the can is filled. The last layer should finish with the remaining cheese.

Place the skillet and can on the grill and close the lid. Cook for about 15 minutes, or until all the cheese is melted.

Remove the skillet and can from the grill. Run a knife around the edge of the can to loosen the nachos. Carefully remove the can by lifting it up, leaving the nacho stack piled on the skillet.

In a microwave, heat the white queso for 1½ minutes, then stir. Ladle the queso over the top of the nacho stack. Garnish with green onions.

YIELD: 6 servings

Chapter 2
VEGETABLES AND SIDES

BARBECUE CHICKEN CHOPPED SALAD
KYLE RUDOLPH

Not only is Kyle Rudolph a powerhouse on the field as a tight end for the NFL, a powerhouse in the NFL, but in his spare time he brings his talents to the backyard grill and serving the community. This is one of his family's favorite recipes.

2 boneless, skinless chicken breasts

¼ cup olive oil

1 tablespoon Operation BBQ Relief Texas SPG Rub or your favorite rub

2 tablespoons Operation BBQ Relief Sweet & Smoky Rub or your favorite rub

2 heads romaine lettuce, chopped

½ cup ranch dressing, divided

2 ears grilled fresh corn, cut from the cob

1 avocado, pitted, peeled, and chopped

1 seedless English cucumber, chopped

1 medium-sized Roma tomato, diced

2 large hard-boiled eggs, chopped

½ cup shredded cheddar cheese

FRIED ONION STRINGS

1 medium yellow onion

1 cup buttermilk

2 teaspoons hot sauce

1 cup all-purpose flour

2 cups vegetable oil, for frying

2 teaspoons Operation BBQ Relief Texas SPG Rub or your favorite rub

2 tablespoons sliced green onions, green and white parts

2 tablespoons barbecue sauce or Homemade Barbecue Sauce (page 165)

Place the chicken breasts, olive oil, and Operation BBQ Relief Texas SPG Rub in an airtight plastic container and allow to marinate overnight and refrigerated.

The next day, remove the chicken from the marinade and discard the marinade. Sprinkle both sides of the chicken with the Operation BBQ Relief Sweet & Smoky Rub.

Preheat a grill to 350°F. Place the chicken on the grill and cook the chicken to an internal temperature of 165°F, about 3 minutes on each side. Remove the chicken from the grill and let it rest for 5 minutes. Then chop it and set it aside.

Place a 5-inch-wide ring mold on a plate.

Mix the lettuce with 2 tablespoons of the ranch dressing. Place the lettuce in the bottom of the ring mold and tamp lightly.

Place the corn, avocado, cucumber, tomato, eggs, cheese, and chicken in a large bowl. Toss with the remaining 6 tablespoons of ranch dressing. Place the mixture on top of the lettuce in the ring mold and tamp lightly. Place ring mold in the refrigerator while cooking the onion strings.

To make the onion strings, trim the ends off the onion and peel off the skin. Standing the onion on the cut side, cut it in half, forming two half-moon-shaped pieces. Place the large cut side of the onion flat on a cutting board and slice the onion into ⅛-inch-thick half-moon slices.

Place the onion strings in a medium bowl and add the buttermilk and hot sauce. Mix well to ensure the onion strings are coated completely. Let the onions marinate for 10 minutes.

Place the flour in a separate medium bowl.

Remove the onions from the marinade and discard the marinade. Add the onions to the flour. Coat the onion strings well and shake off the excess flour.

Add at least 1 inch of oil to a medium pot on the stove. Heat the oil over medium heat and use a thermometer to check that it does not exceed 350°F.

Continued

Fry the onions in batches of 4 for about 2 minutes, turning halfway through. When the onions are golden brown, remove them from the pot and drain them on a paper towel–lined plate.

Place the onions on a cookie sheet and season with rub.

Carefully remove the salad from the ring mold onto a serving platter. Place the onion strings in a pile on top of the salad. Sprinkle the green onions on top of the onion strings. Drizzle the top of the salad with barbecue sauce and serve.

YIELD: 2 servings

OLD-SCHOOL GREEN BEANS FOR THE PARTY

JOEY SMITH

You can't have a barbecue without green beans, and these are delicious! These green beans become more of a casserole as you add the chicken soup and cheese to them. Throw in some bacon and these green beans are the perfect side dish at any barbecue!

1 (10-pound) can green beans, drained

1 large white onion, chopped

1 pound bacon, cooked and chopped

1 (10-ounce) can cream of chicken soup

6 large jalapeños, minced

1 tablespoon black pepper

1 pound Velveeta, cut into 1-inch cubes

Preheat an oven or smoker to 350°F.

Combine the green beans, onion, bacon, soup, jalapeños, and pepper in a large bowl. Mix well, then transfer in a 9 by 13-inch metal baking dish.

Place the baking dish in the oven or smoker and cook for 1½ hours, or until the onions are tender.

Remove the casserole and sprinkle the cheese on top. Cover and return to the oven for 5 minutes. Stir, then serve.

YIELD: 12 to 16 servings

TEXAS CHROME MASH

JOEY SMITH

Who knew mashed potatoes could be packed with so much flavor? Take your mashed potatoes to a new level by adding the Mexican flavors of green chiles, salsa verde, and cilantro.

4 large russet potatoes, peeled and chopped into 1-inch dice

¼ cup chopped mild green chiles

½ teaspoon taco seasoning

1 ounce cream cheese

½ cup salsa verde

½ cup green enchilada sauce

¼ cup chopped fresh cilantro

¼ cup chopped green onions, green and white parts

½ cup Mexican crema

½ cup shredded Monterey jack cheese

2 tablespoons unsalted butter, softened

1 teaspoon Texas Chrome BBQ Rub or your favorite rub

1 teaspoon Texas Chrome GPS or a mixture of garlic, salt, and pepper

Place the potatoes in a large pot and cover with water. Boil the potatoes over medium heat for about 10 minutes, or until they are soft.

While the potatoes are cooking, mix the remaining ingredients in a large bowl.

Once soft, drain the potatoes. Add the potatoes into the bowl and mash to combine them with the other ingredients. Mix well and serve.

YIELD: 6 to 8 servings

CORN PUDDING

TREY WINGO

Corn is a classic side dish for any barbecue, but this recipe takes it to the next level. The sugar and butter are easy additions that pack a lot of extra flavor. The extra sweetness and richness make this the perfect comfort food dish!

¼ cup (½ stick) unsalted butter, plus 1 tablespoon, softened, to grease the dish

¼ cup all-purpose flour

1 teaspoon kosher salt

1½ tablespoons sugar

1¾ cups milk

3 cups frozen corn

3 large eggs

Place the butter in a large saucepan over medium heat to melt, stirring constantly. Then add the flour, salt, and sugar and cook for about 1 minute, or until bubbly.

Add the milk slowly, stirring constantly until the consistency is smooth and thick.

Remove from the heat and stir in the corn to cool the mixture.

In a separate 1-quart bowl, beat the eggs until frothy, then fold them into the mixture.

Grease a 9 by 13-inch casserole dish with the softened butter.

Preheat the oven to 350°F. Place the casserole dish in a larger pan and add about 1 inch of water. Bake the casserole dish and larger pan for about 45 minutes, or until the center of the pudding no longer jiggles. Remove the casserole from the oven and let it cool slightly before serving.

YIELD: 6 servings

PARMALEE FAMILY SLAMMIN' POTATO SALAD

BERNIE PARMALEE

This recipe has been in the Parmalee family for years. During that time, they have added a dab of this and subtracted a dash of that. They've perfected it to a family tradition, and this dish is at every barbecue they have! This can also be prepared a day early to help save time.

1 (5-pound) bag red potatoes, skin on

12 large eggs

1 (16-ounce) jar kosher dill pickles

2 to 3 stalks celery, finely chopped

1 (15-ounce) jar real mayonnaise

2 tablespoons dry mustard

1 teaspoon Lawry's Seasoned Salt

¼ teaspoon smoked paprika

Place the potatoes in a large pot and bring to a boil. Cook them until tender, then drain and let cool. While the potatoes are cooking, prepare the eggs. Place the eggs in a large pan and cover with 1 inch water above the eggs. Turn the heat to high. Once the eggs come to a rapid boil, turn off the heat and leave the pot covered for 10 minutes. Once they are done, drain and let cool, then peel and chop.

Once the potatoes are cool, peel off the skins and cut the potatoes into small dice. Place them in a large serving bowl to be used for the potato salad.

Next, drain the juice from the pickle jar. Place the pickles in a food chopper or processor and finely chop. Add them, along with the celery and eggs, to the bowl with the potatoes.

Add ½ the jar of mayonnaise. Mix well. If you need more, add ½ cup at a time until you reach the desired consistency and wetness.

Add the dry mustard. Stir well. Add the seasoned salt. Stir well and taste. Add more to reach the desired level of seasoning. Sprinkle the top with paprika.

Store covered in the refrigerator until ready to serve.

YIELD: 12 servings

LOBSTER PASTA SALAD
KURT AND BRENDA WARNER

Enjoy this delicious lobster pasta salad recipe from Pro Football Hall of Fame Quarterback Kurt Warner and his wife, Brenda. The dedicant lobster chunks add a richness to a light pasta salad side and truly make it a championship dish.

6 ounces orecchiette or small shell pasta

DRESSING

¾ cup real mayonnaise

1 cup barbecue sauce

Salt and freshly ground black pepper

1 tablespoon tarragon vinegar

2 cups lobster meat, cut into bite-size chunks (two 1¼-pound lobsters)

1 cup diced celery

2 cups shredded sharp cheddar cheese

½ cup thinly sliced green onions, green and white parts

2 tablespoons chopped fresh tarragon, or 2 teaspoons dried tarragon, crumbled

Cook the pasta according to the directions on the package, until firm. Drain it in a colander and rinse briefly under cold water. Drain it completely and set aside.

To make the dressing, place all the ingredients in a small bowl and whisk to combine.

Place the pasta in a large bowl and add the lobster, celery, cheese, green onion, and tarragon. Gently toss.

Pour the dressing over the mixture and gently toss again. Cover and refrigerate for 1 to 8 hours. If the salad is refrigerated for 8 hours or more, a small amount of mayonnaise may need to be added.

Serve chilled.

YIELD: 4 to 6 servings

MAMA JUNE'S FAMOUS BAKED BEANS

NICK WOOLFOLK

Mama June's famous Mississippi Delta baked beans have been served from New York to Australia and everywhere in between! These baked beans are so much more than warming up a can of beans. Adding the meat, onion, and bell pepper, along with some additional spices and sauces, will make these beans rich and hearty. A great side dish for any summer barbecue!

½ small yellow onion, chopped

½ red bell pepper, seeded and chopped

½ pound cooked beef or pork, chopped

48 ounces your favorite canned baked beans, drained

3 tablespoons yellow mustard

6 teaspoons light brown sugar

2 tablespoons Worcestershire sauce

2 tablespoons barbecue sauce

2 tablespoons Operation BBQ Relief Sweet & Smoky Rub or your favorite barbecue seasoning

Place the onion and bell pepper in a large sauté pan over medium-high heat. Sauté for about 15 minutes, or until translucent and aromatic. Add the meat and cook for 3 minutes. Set aside.

Combine the beans, mustard, brown sugar, Worcestershire sauce, barbecue sauce, and rub in a large heatproof dish. Add the peppers, onion, and meat and mix well.

Preheat a smoker to 300°F. Place the dish, uncovered, in the smoker and cook for about 1 hour and 15 minutes, or until the beans reach a temperature of 160°F internally.

Remove the dish from the smoker and allow it to cool for 15 minutes before serving.

YIELD: 10 to 12 servings

BACON-WRAPPED ASPARAGUS
JOHNNY IMBRIOLO

This quick and easy side is packed with a great smoky bacon flavor and deep charred asparagus—a great way to eat your vegetables! By using a cast-iron skillet, so much extra flavor is added to the asparagus. The cast-iron skillets are "seasoned" with more use, so the more you use your skillet, the better your food will taste!

1 bunch medium asparagus

1 tablespoon olive oil

2 teaspoons Operation BBQ Relief Texas SPG Rub or your favorite rub

3 slices hickory-smoked bacon

1 tablespoon julienned carrots, for garnish

Take 6 asparagus spears and bunch them together so that the tips are even. Cut off 2 inches from the bottom of the asparagus. Repeat this with all the asparagus. Coat the cut asparagus with oil and rub.

Starting at the bottom of the bunch, wrap the bacon around the asparagus toward the top.

Turn your grill to high and preheat a medium cast-iron skillet.

Place the asparagus in the heated cast-iron skillet and cook for 3 to 4 minutes, until the bacon starts to get crispy. Continue to rotate the asparagus and cook until the bacon has become crispy on all sides. Remove the asparagus from the pan.

Garnish the top with the carrots and serve.

YIELD: 3 servings

MAC 'N' CHEESE

MIKE GOLIC JR.

Mac 'n' cheese is a must-have at a barbecue. This recipe is all about the cheese! The Gruyère adds a sweet and slightly salty flavor, the sharp cheddar packs a zing, the Gouda brings a sweetness, and the pepper jack has a subtle note of spice.

1 pound cavatappi pasta, partially cooked

½ cup (1 stick) unsalted butter, plus 2 tablespoons melted

3 tablespoons all-purpose flour

3 cups half and half

2 ounces cream cheese

1 cup shredded sharp cheddar

1 cup shredded pepper jack

1 cup shredded Gruyère

1½ cups shredded Gouda

3 tablespoons panko bread crumbs

2 tablespoons sliced green onion, green and white parts, for garnish

2 teaspoons diced tomato, for garnish

Place the pasta in a large cast-iron skillet.

Place a large saucepot over medium heat on the stove. Add the butter and let it melt. Once melted, add the flour and stir, making sure there are no lumps.

Cook the butter and flour for about 1 minute to remove the raw flour flavor. Add the half and half and stir until the butter/flour mix is emulsified.

Add the cream cheese, cheddar, pepper jack, Gruyere, and Gouda. Continue to stir until the cheese is completely melted and the sauce is formed. Make sure the cheese sauce does not stick to the bottom of the pot.

Pour the sauce over the pasta and mix well in the skillet. Sprinkle the top with bread crumbs and drizzle the melted butter over the bread crumbs.

Set a smoker to 250°F. Place the skillet in the smoker and cook for about 20 minutes, or until the bread crumbs start to turn brown. Remove the skillet from the smoker and sprinkle the top of the casserole with the green onions and tomato before serving.

YIELD: 4 servings

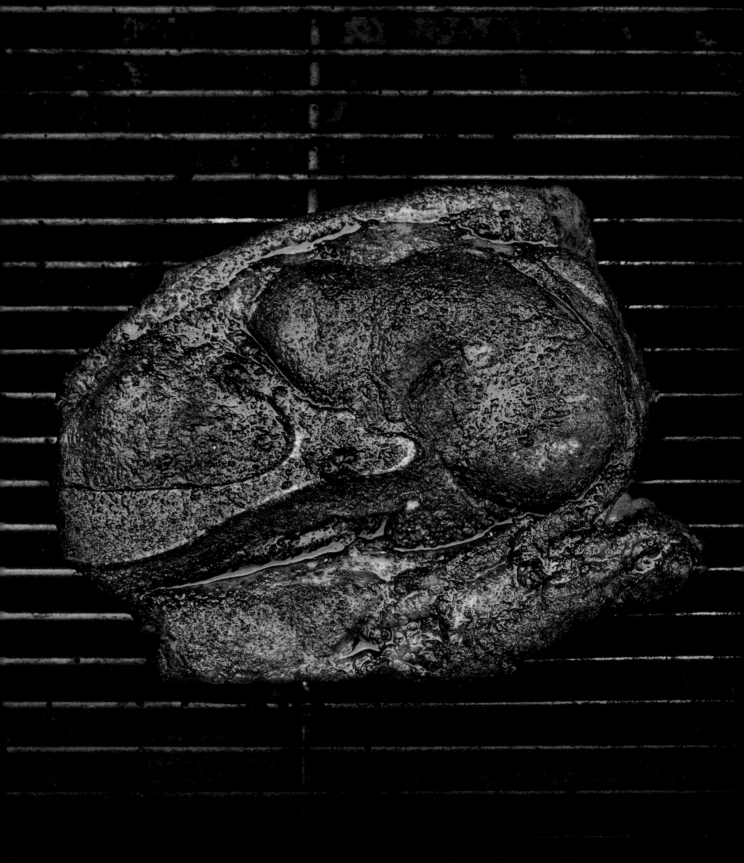

Chapter 3
PORK

SIGNATURE PORK TENDERLOIN

MITCH SCHWARTZ

Former NFL offensive tackle for the Kansas City Chiefs and Super Bowl Champion Mitch Schwartz shows off his cooking skills with this quick, but delicious, pork tenderloin recipe. With the combination of the honey and balsamic, the pork takes on sweet and tangy flavors that are complemented by the flavor of rosemary.

1 twin pack Prairie Fresh pork tenderloin (each tenderloin 12 to 14 ounces)

2 teaspoons Operation BBQ Relief Texas SPG Rub or your favorite rub

2 teaspoons Operation BBQ Relief Cajun Bayou Rub or your favorite rub

⅔ cup balsamic vinegar

8 ounces minced garlic

½ cup honey

Sprig of rosemary

Light a charcoal chimney filled with charcoal.

Remove the tenderloins from their packaging and use a sharp knife to remove the silver skin.

Sprinkle the Texas SPG Rub over both tenderloins, then add the Cajun Bayou Rub. Add additional Cajun rub if you prefer extra spice. Let the tenderloins rest.

Place the vinegar, garlic, and honey in a medium-sized metal saucepan over medium heat. Add the rosemary to the liquid once hot. Be careful not to burn it. Continue to stir the mixture until it is combined and begins to reduce. Remove the pan from the heat and let it cool. Remove the rosemary.

Put the charcoal from the chimney in the grill. Grill the tenderloins over direct heat, turning every 2 to 3 minutes. Start to baste the tenderloins with the honey-balsamic glaze once the temperature of the meat is over 125°F to 130°F. Reserve some of the glaze for serving.

Cook the tenderloin to an internal temperature of 140°F to 150°F in the thickest part. It will become a dark, golden brown. Once the tenderloin hits this temperature, remove it from the grill and cover loosely with aluminum foil. Let it rest for 5 to 10 minutes, then slice. Use the remaining glaze for sauce when serving.

YIELD: 6 servings

SYMON'S RIBS
MICHAEL SYMON

Most people don't think about cooking their meat with pickle juice. Famed chef Michael Symon, however, shows how to use the tangy pickle flavors by complementing them with brown sugar.

PORK RUB
⅓ cup kosher salt

⅓ cup black pepper

2 tablespoons celery seed

2 tablespoons ground coriander

1 tablespoon smoked paprika

PORK
2 (3 to 4-pound) slabs pork spareribs

1 cup Pork Rub

2 cups firmly packed light brown sugar

1 cup dill pickle juice

Prepare and preheat a smoker to 300°F.

To make the rub, place all the ingredients in a small bowl and mix. Set aside.

Remove the white membrane from the ribs. Pat the ribs dry with paper towels and season both sides with the rub. Any extra rub can be stored in an airtight container for up to 1 month.

In a large saucepan, whisk together the brown sugar and pickle juice. Heat over medium-high heat, stirring until the sugar has completely dissolved, about 5 minutes. Remove from the heat and set aside.

When the temperature in the smoker reaches 300°F and the smoke is running clear, add the ribs bone side down. After 1½ hours, test the ribs for doneness by flipping a rack and pressing the meat between the bones. If the meat pulls away from the bones, it's done. If not, continue smoking until it does, about 30 minutes more.

When the ribs are done, gently brush them with the glaze, being careful not to remove the bark that forms on the exterior of the meat. Cut between the bones and serve with your favorite barbecue sauce if you prefer.

YIELD: 8 servings

RICKIE'S FAVORITE BABY BACK RIBS

RICKIE FOWLER

This recipe delivers the perfect plate of ribs. Professional golfer Rickie Fowler thinks these ribs are delicious, even without any barbecue sauce!

2 full racks pork baby back ribs, each cut in half crosswise

3 teaspoons sea salt

6 lemons, halved

Heat a grill to between 300°F and 350°F—make sure not to go above 350°F or flames might occur.

Season the ribs with 1 teaspoon salt, ¼ teaspoon per half rack. Place the ribs directly on the grill, bone side down, and cook for 3 minutes. Turn the ribs over every 3 minutes. The ribs will cook for a total of 21 minutes. Alternate the seasoning with each turn. For the first turn, season with salt. For the second turn, season with squeezed lemon. The ribs are done when the internal temperature reaches 160°F.

Once finished, remove the rib racks from the grill and place on a cutting board. Slice into individual ribs and serve, either dry or with your favorite barbecue sauce.

YIELD: 4 servings

TEQUILA BARBECUE SPARERIBS
GUY FIERI

Tequila is such a unique addition to any barbecue marinade or sauce. Food Network star Guy Fieri shows how to best highlight the tequila flavor while complementing it with dried chiles and freshly squeezed lime juice.

SAUCE

1 California/New Mexico dried chile

¼ cup hot water

1 (6-ounce) can tomato paste

1 cup firmly packed light brown sugar

½ cup Santo Blanco tequila

¼ cup freshly squeezed lime juice

1 tablespoon minced garlic

1 tablespoon molasses

Salt and freshly ground black pepper

RIBS

4 pounds pork spareribs, cut St. Louis-style

RUB

2 tablespoons ground cumin

2 tablespoons garlic powder

2 tablespoons onion powder

2 tablespoons smoked paprika

2 tablespoons kosher salt

2 teaspoons black pepper

1 teaspoon ancho chili powder

To make the sauce, place the dried chile in a medium bowl with the hot water to rehydrate. Let it soak for 10 minutes.

In a medium saucepan, add the tomato paste, brown sugar, tequila, lime juice, garlic, and molasses. Stir well and bring to a gentle simmer over medium heat.

Add the rehydrated chile and soaking water to the saucepan, season with salt and pepper, and simmer for about 3 minutes, or until the flavors blend together. Pour into a blender and process until smooth, and set aside. Serve with the ribs as a dipping sauce or baste them with the mixture during cooking.

Preheat the oven to 275°F.

To prepare the ribs, begin by trimming any excess fat or sinew. Remove the thin membrane from the back side of the ribs and discard. To make the rub, combine all the ingredients in a small bowl.

Lay out a few large sheets of aluminum foil (one for each slab). Place 1 rack on each sheet and divide the dry rub between each slab. Rub the mixture into the ribs on both sides and then fold the foil over to form a sealed pouch around each rack. At this stage, make sure the racks are meat side down. Place each foil pouch on a large roasting tray and bake in the oven for 2 hours.

After 2 hours, open the foil and peel it back so the ribs are exposed. Carefully turn the racks over so they are meat side up. Then cook for 1½ hours more with the foil open. When done, the ribs will be tender, and the meat will have shrunk back from the bones. Baste the ribs with the sauce and caramelize them on a grill or under the broiler for 1 to 2 minutes to add more color.

YIELD: 4 to 6 servings

BIG BOY PORK STEAK

DEWAYNE DANIEL

Cooking a pork steak can be done by anyone—even a grilling novice! Using your favorite rubs, marinades, and sauces can help make this meal your own. Champion pitmaster Dewayne Daniel shares his favorite flavor combinations here!

1 (¼-inch-thick) pork steak, cut out of a Boston butt

Strawberry's rub or your favorite rub

½ cup Wicker's marinade or your favorite marinade

4 tablespoons Blues Hog Champions' Blend BBQ Sauce or your favorite barbecue sauce

Apply a light coating of rub to both sides of the steak. Let it sit on the counter for 30 minutes to start sweating, then apply a heavier coat of rub. Allow the steak to come all the way up to room temperature before heading toward the grill.

Heat a grill to 250°F. Place the steak in the indirect cooking zone. Cook it for 1 hour, flip, then cook for another hour. Remove the steak from the grill and place it on a piece of aluminum foil. Top with the marinade, then seal.

Cook for 1½ hours in the foil, then unwrap. Baste the steak with the barbecue sauce, then grill for 3 minutes. Flip the steak, baste again, and grill for 3 minutes more.

Remove the steak from the grill and let it rest for 10 minutes before serving.

YIELD: 1 serving

PAN-FRIED SMOKED PORK CHOP

REGGIE BROOKS

For those of you who like pan-fried pork chops, you are going to love this recipe. It adds just a hint of smoke to a crispy pan-fried pork chop with slow-cooked onions and potatoes. You won't be disappointed!

Hickory chips for smoking

1 (1-pound) bone-in, thick-cut rack pork chop

1 teaspoon canola oil

¾ teaspoon kosher salt, divided

⅜ teaspoon black pepper, divided

1 tablespoon unsalted butter

½ cup thinly sliced (1⁄16 inch) yellow onion

3 Yukon gold potatoes, skin on, sliced

4 medium button mushrooms, stemmed

1 cup all-purpose flour

1 cup panko bread crumbs

1 cup beaten eggs (about 4 large eggs)

2 tablespoons canola oil, for frying

1 sprig fresh rosemary, for garnish

Preheat a smoker to 175°F and add the hickory chips.

Rub the pork chop with oil and season with ¼ teaspoon of the salt and ⅛ teaspoon of the pepper on both sides. Place it in the smoker, with heavy smoke, for 10 minutes. Remove the pork chop from the smoker and place it in the refrigerator to cool.

While the pork chop is cooling, heat a large cast-iron skillet on the grill and add the butter, onions, potatoes, and mushroom caps. Season with the remaining ½ teaspoon salt and ¼ teaspoon pepper and cook for about 15 minutes, turning often until the vegetables are golden brown. Set aside, separating the potatoes and onions from the mushrooms.

Remove the pork chop from the refrigerator. Split the chop in half lengthwise toward the bone, but do not fully separate the pork (it should look like a butterfly). Using a meat mallet, gently pound both sides of the pork chop until the pork chop is approximately ½-inch thick. Place the flour and bread crumbs on separate plates and place the eggs in a bowl. First dip the pork chop in flour, then dip in egg, and finally dredge in the bread crumbs to coat on both sides.

Prepare a grill to 350°F. Place a large cast-iron skillet on the grill and add the oil. When the oil reaches 350°F, place the breaded pork chop into the pan. Cook for about 2 minutes on each side, or until the internal temperature reaches 140°F.

Place the potatoes and onions on a large plate, piling as high as possible. Lean the pork chop on top of the vegetables. Place the mushrooms on top of the pork chop and garnish with the rosemary sprig.

YIELD: 1 serving

BARBECUE BABY BACK PORK RIBS

This family-style meal was a staple at the Bleier family restaurant in Wisconsin. Bleier's Bar was started by Rocky Bleier's parents in 1945, and by the mid-'50s, they started serving food. Their first foray into the food business started with Friday night fish dinner, which morphed into Saturday night chicken and rib dinners.

RUB

1 cup sugar

¼ cup kosher salt

¼ cup smoked paprika

RIBS

3 racks pork ribs (ideal thickness of 1¾ down)

2 tablespoons water

¼ cup apple cider vinegar

1 cup barbecue sauce

To make the rub, place all the ingredients in a small bowl and mix. Rub the mixture on both sides of the ribs and let them rest for 30 minutes.

Preheat an oven to 350°F.

Place the ribs meat side down on a large tray and add the water to the tray. Cover the tray with aluminum foil and place it in the oven. Cook for 1 hour. Remove the tray from the oven and flip the ribs over, meat side up. Sprinkle the ribs with vinegar. Re-cover the ribs with foil and bake them for about 1 more hour, or until they are dark brown.

Remove the ribs from the oven and coat them with your favorite barbecue sauce before serving.

YIELD: 6 servings

BARBECUE PULLED PORK FLATBREAD

There are so many ways to enjoy pulled pork—why not enjoy it on a pizza? This recipe delivers all the flavors of pulled pork while being easy to enjoy! This handheld meal is super easy to make, so it is perfect for kids who want to get involved in the kitchen.

1 prebaked flatbread or naan bread (about 9 by 7 inches)

2 tablespoons barbecue sauce

2 ounces shredded Monterey jack cheese

2 ounces smoked pulled pork

1 teaspoon Operation BBQ Relief Sweet & Smoky Rub or your favorite rub

1 teaspoon finely sliced green onion, white and green parts

Preheat a grill to 350°F.

Place the flatbread on a large cutting board. Spread the barbecue sauce evenly over the flatbread, leaving a ¼-inch rim around the edge.

Add the cheese over the barbecue sauce. Evenly spread the pulled pork over the cheese. Sprinkle the rub over the pork.

Transfer the flatbread to a large cookie sheet and place it on the grill over indirect heat. Make sure the flatbread is on the cooler side of the grill. Cook the flatbread for 10 to 15 minutes, until crispy.

Remove the flatbread from the grill and slice it into 8 equal pieces. Sprinkle the green onions over the top of the flatbread.

YIELD: 4 servings

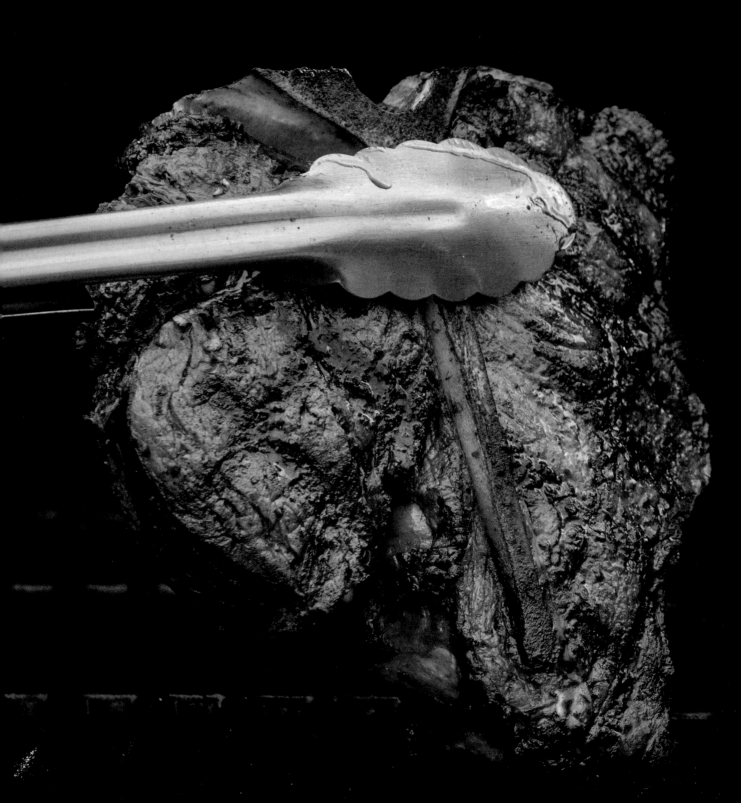

Chapter 4
BEEF AND LAMB

KOREAN BARBECUE SHORT RIBS ON COKE

This is a classic Korean barbecue recipe with a twist. Tila was taught that the secret to tender grilled short ribs is using apple pear and Coca-Cola because they help break down the beef. KBBQ pros love the slightly chewy texture of flanken-cut short ribs, but it's not for all. If that makes you cringe a little, use any steak cut of beef like flank, New York strip, or even rib eye.

MARINADE

¼ cup soy sauce

¼ cup Coca-Cola Classic

3 tablespoons light brown sugar

2 cloves garlic, finely minced

1 apple pear, halved, peeled, and grated on a box grater

1 tablespoon toasted sesame oil

RIBS

2 pounds flanken-cut short ribs

TOPPINGS

1 tablespoon toasted sesame seeds, for garnish

2 green onions, very finely sliced on an angle, for garnish

To make the marinade, place all the ingredients in a large bowl. Using a whisk or fork, stir until the sugar is dissolved and the garlic is distributed evenly.

Add the ribs to the bowl and massage the marinade into the beef. Cover and allow the meat to marinate for 1 to 4 hours.

Heat a grill to high for at least 5 minutes. If using a charcoal or gas grill, wipe the grill grates down with a lightly oiled towel right before cooking to clean any char and debris. This will give a great grill mark and help keep the beef from sticking.

Pat any excess marinade off the ribs using a paper towel. Grill for about 4 minutes on each side, or until desired doneness is achieved. Remove the ribs from the grill and garnish them with sesame seeds and green onions before serving.

YIELD: 4 servings

LAMB SHEESH! KEBABS
AARTI SEQUERIA

One of the best kinds of kebabs are the ones made of ground meat. They're usually more tender than those made with chunks of meat and more flavorful to your palate. In Turkish, these are called shish kebabs, hence the tongue-in-cheek name for this version. Aarti made these during *Food Network Star* for some of the legends, and he remembers his hands trembling so much that when he was preparing them, he cut himself.

1 pound ground lamb

½-inch piece ginger

2 large cloves garlic

2 medium shallots, peeled and coarsely chopped

1 tablespoon freshly grated lemon zest

4 sprigs mint

¾ teaspoon kosher salt

4 tablespoons pomegranate molasses, divided

½ teaspoon baking soda

¼ teaspoon garam masala

2 teaspoons black pepper

1 teaspoon sunflower oil

8 metal skewers

2 tablespoons freshly squeezed lemon juice

Bring the lamb to room temperature. Meanwhile, place the ginger, garlic, shallots, lemon zest, mint, cilantro, and salt in a food processor and chop until finely minced, then move to a large bowl.

Add the lamb, 2 tablespoons of the pomegranate molasses, baking soda, garam masala, and pepper to the large bowl. Using your hands, knead for 2 to 5 minutes, until the meat lightens in color.

Divide the meat into 8 equal portions.

Drizzle the sunflower oil onto a large platter for the kebabs. Take a ball of meat and roll it into a short stump. Thread the skewer through it, then begin shaping the kebab along the length of the skewer using quick, light strokes. The meat should be about ¼ inch thick. Repeat with 1 to 2 more balls of meat depending upon the length of your skewer. Lay the completed kebab on your oiled platter and repeat with the rest of the skewers and lamb.

Preheat a griddle over medium heat. Drizzle oil over it; when it starts to smoke, it's ready. Meanwhile, to make a glaze, mix the lemon juice with the remaining 2 tablespoons pomegranate molasses in a small bowl.

Lay the skewers on the hot griddle and cook for about 2 minutes. Rotate a quarter turn and cook for another 2 minutes. Continue this way until the skewers have cooked a total of 8 to 10 minutes. On the last turn, brush the surface of the kebabs with glaze.

Remove the kebabs from the griddle to your serving platter and serve immediately.

YIELD: 4 servings

MEZCAL-MARINATED SKIRT STEAK ASADA

ARIEL FOX

This skirt steak is perfect for tacos! The mezcal alcohol works beautifully to help tenderize the meat before cooking it. Use a little bit of guacamole, some salsa, and a grilled tortilla with this incredibly flavorful meat to have the perfect Mexican meal.

MARINADE

1 teaspoon chili flakes

6 cloves garlic, finely grated

¼ cup freshly squeezed orange juice

2 tablespoons gluten-free, low-sodium soy sauce

1 tablespoon coconut aminos

½ cup freshly squeezed lime juice

¾ cup mezcal

¼ cup Maggi seasoning sauce

2 teaspoons dried oregano, preferably Mexican

1 teaspoon ground cumin

1 teaspoon sea salt

MEAT

2 pounds outside skirt steak

2 tablespoons olive oil

¼ teaspoon sea salt

¼ teaspoon black pepper

Guacamole, for serving

Salsa, for serving

Grilled tortillas, for serving

To make the marinade, place all the ingredients in a medium bowl and whisk to combine. Place the steak in a resealable plastic bag and pour in the marinade. Seal tightly and marinate for 2 to 8 hours in the refrigerator.

Prepare a wood/charcoal grill to high heat. Make sure the grill is clean and seasoned. Season the steak with salt and pepper. Grill the steak over high heat, turning occasionally until charred, 2 to 3 minutes per side for medium-rare. Transfer it to a cooling rack or cutting board and let it rest for 10 minutes. Slice against the grain into ½-inch-thick strips.

Serve this steak with freshly made guacamole, salsa, and grilled tortillas for wrapping. This steak is so flavorful you don't need much more than that!

YIELD: 4 servings

SOUTHWEST BRISKET CHILI

MIKE GOLIC

What is better than a can of beer with your chili? How about adding that beer to your chili? This recipe calls for your favorite lager to be added to the recipe. This secret ingredient will add a unique flavor combination to a hearty brisket chili full of Southwest spices.

1 tablespoon canola oil

1 pound ground beef

2 tablespoons kosher salt, divided

1 cup diced yellow onion

½ ounce chopped garlic

1½ ounces minced jalapeño, seeded

4 ounces seeded, diced green pepper

2 slices pepper bacon, cooked and diced

1 pound smoked brisket, diced

1¼ cups Shiner Bock beer or your favorite lager

2 cups canned crushed tomatoes, with juices

1 tablespoon light brown sugar

1 tablespoon chopped chipotle peppers in adobo sauce

½ teaspoon smoked paprika

2 tablespoons ground cumin

½ teaspoon chicken base

1½ cups water

Tortilla chips, for serving

Place the oil in a large saucepot over high heat. Add the ground beef and sprinkle with 1 tablespoon of the kosher salt. Stir frequently to break up the meat until it's browned.

Remove the ground beef using a slotted spoon, leaving the oil in the pot, and set the beef aside.

Add the onion, garlic, jalapeño, and green pepper to the pot with the oil. Sauté over medium heat for about 5 minutes, or until the onions become translucent and the peppers become tender.

Add the ground beef, bacon, and brisket to the pot and stir. Add the beer, tomatoes, brown sugar, chipotle peppers, paprika, cumin, chicken base, and water.

Lower the heat to a simmer and cook for 30 minutes.

Turn off the heat, taste, and add the remaining tablespoon of salt if needed. This dish is great served with tortilla chips.

YIELD: 8 servings

BOURBON–BARBECUE BEEF BACK RIBS

MICHAEL OLLIER

Sriracha, bourbon, and soy sauce give these beef back ribs a sweet and spicy flavor that's absolutely divine. While the recipe calls for these items only in small amounts, they pack a punch of flavor. Barbecue sauce adds to the depth of these ribs, which are perfect for any backyard barbecue.

2 racks Certified Angus Beef back ribs

2 tablespoons kosher salt

4 teaspoons black pepper

1 cup barbecue sauce

¼ cup bourbon

1 tablespoon soy sauce

1 tablespoon hot chili sauce

Preheat a smoker to 250°F.

Trim excess fat and remove the thin membrane from the bone side of the back ribs. Season the ribs evenly with salt and pepper. Place them in the smoker, meat side up, and smoke for 2½ to 3 hours, to reach an internal temperature of 200°F, then set aside.

In a small saucepan, combine the barbecue sauce, bourbon, soy sauce, and chili sauce. Bring to a boil over high heat while stirring. Then lower the heat to a simmer and cook for about 5 minutes more.

Preheat the oven broiler to high.

Glaze the rib meat with sauce, then place it under the broiler for 3 to 5 minutes, until the ribs begin to bubble.

Slice into individual ribs and serve.

YIELD: 3 to 4 servings

GRILLED CAESAR SALAD with HERB-BUTTER STEAK

BRYAN MROCZKA

Take a classic dish and add some flair by preparing it on a grill. Once the charred texture of the leafy greens and steak combine with the creamy Caesar dressing, croutons, and Parmesan cheese, you will realize it's the perfect dish.

HERB BUTTER

½ cup (1 stick) unsalted butter, room temperature

¼ teaspoon minced garlic

1 teaspoon minced fresh dill

1 tablespoon chopped flat leaf parsley

1 teaspoon freshly squeezed lemon juice

1 teaspoon kosher salt

¼ teaspoon black pepper

DRESSING

2 cloves garlic, finely chopped

2 tablespoons freshly squeezed lemon juice

2 teaspoons Dijon mustard

2 teaspoons Worcestershire sauce

1 cup real mayonnaise

1 teaspoon anchovy paste

¼ teaspoon black pepper

⅓ cup olive oil

½ cup shredded Parmesan cheese

CROUTONS

1 baguette or Italian bread loaf, sliced

1 teaspoon olive oil

Salt and freshly ground black pepper

SALAD

1 teaspoon olive oil

2 hearts of romaine lettuce

½ teaspoon kosher salt

½ teaspoon black pepper

STEAK

4 (1-inch-thick) prime rib eyes

2 teaspoons olive oil

2 teaspoons kosher salt

1 teaspoon black pepper

Preheat a grill to medium-high heat.

To make the herb butter, place all the ingredients in a medium bowl and mix. Spoon the butter mixture onto a piece of plastic wrap and roll so the butter forms a log. Place it in the refrigerator so the butter hardens.

To make the dressing, mix the garlic, lemon juice, mustard, Worcestershire, mayonnaise, anchovy paste, and pepper in a separate medium bowl. Slowly whisk in the olive oil. Add the Parmesan and continue to whisk. Refrigerate the dressing until it's time to serve the salad.

Continued

SMOKED CHUCK ROAST
MICHAEL OLLIER

This cut is traditionally used for a pot roast, but smoking it instead of using a traditional braise yields a different eating experience altogether. Sit back, let the smoker do the work for you, and get ready for the best pulled beef you've ever tasted.

1 tablespoon yellow mustard

2 teaspoons dill pickle juice

3 pounds Certified Angus Beef chuck roast

1 tablespoon kosher salt

1½ teaspoons coarsely ground black pepper, dustless preferred

Place the mustard and pickle juice in a small bowl and stir to combine. Coat the entire surface of the chuck roast with the mustard mixture. Season the roast evenly with salt and pepper, making sure to fully coat the sides, top, and bottom. Fit a large sheet pan with a wire rack and place the roast on top. Refrigerate overnight, uncovered and away from ready-to-eat food.

The next day, preheat a smoker to 275°F. Place the chuck roast directly from the refrigerator into the smoker and smoke until an internal temperature of 180°F is reached, 5 to 6 hours. Wrap the roast tightly in two layers of aluminum foil and return it to the smoker for 45 minutes to 1 hour more, until the internal temperature reaches 205°F. Alternately, preheat an oven to 275°F and finish the wrapped chuck roast for the same amount of cooking time.

Remove the roast from the heat and let rest with the foil slightly opened to allow the majority of steam to escape. Pour the liquid from the foil into a container and skim any excess fat from the top. Shred the beef by hand or using two forks, discarding any larger fat chunks. Then toss the meat with the cooking liquid and serve. It is best served as either a sandwich or a taco.

YIELD: 6 to 8 servings

FAMILY-STYLE PORTERHOUSE

MICHAEL OLLIER

The porterhouse is two steaks in one: a tenderloin on one side of the T-bone and strip on the other. Have one cut to 40 ounces and you make a statement: go big or go home! Plan ahead and marinate overnight for the fullest flavor.

1 lemon

1 tablespoon chopped garlic

1 teaspoon kosher salt

½ teaspoon black pepper

1 (40-ounce) Certified Angus Beef porterhouse

2 large sprigs rosemary

1 tablespoon olive oil

½ teaspoon high-quality sea salt, such as Maldon

Using a rasp grater, zest and juice the lemon, reserving the zest for later. Place the lemon juice, garlic, salt, and pepper in a bowl. Place the steak in a large resealable plastic bag and coat the steak evenly with the marinade liquid. Add the rosemary and close tightly, pressing out all the air. Refrigerate overnight.

The next day, preheat a grill to 250°F.

Remove the steak from the marinade and discard the marinade. Wrap the steak in aluminum foil. Place it on the grill, away from direct heat, and cook slowly for 60 to 90 minutes, flipping once halfway through. The internal temperature should reach 100°F. Remove the steak from the grill and increase the heat to 450°F to 500°F. Allow the steak to rest for 15 minutes in the foil while the grill is heating to a higher temperature.

Remove the steak from the foil, pat dry, and brush with oil. Sear 2 to 3 minutes per side for medium-rare, or an internal temperature of 130°F. Transfer to a clean, large cutting board.

Carve the steak by running a knife along the bone to remove both the strip and the tenderloin. Slice each steak in ¼ to ½-inch-thick slices and serve on a large platter. Combine the reserved lemon zest with the sea salt in a small bowl. Garnish the slices of steak with the lemon–sea salt blend and serve.

YIELD: 4 servings

PRIME RIB with HORSERADISH SAUCE

STAN HAYS

By using mayonnaise on the prime rib itself, you lock in the moisture of the meat. It also helps all the spices stick to the meat and not fall off while cooking. Top this prime rib with some homemade horseradish sauce and you have perfectly cooked meat full of flavor!

SAUCE

2 cups real mayonnaise

4 tablespoons Worcestershire sauce

3 tablespoons Weber Roasted Garlic and Herb Seasoning or your favorite garlic seasoning

1 (8-ounce) jar extra-hot prepared horseradish, or 4 to 5 tablespoons grated fresh horseradish

2 teaspoons black pepper

MEAT

1 (6.5-pound) prime rib

½ cup real mayonnaise

4 tablespoons fresh horseradish

1 tablespoon Operation BBQ Relief Texas SPG Rub or your favorite rub

1 tablespoon Operation BBQ Relief Texas Santa Maria Steak Rub or your favorite rub

1-inch piece horseradish root

To make the sauce, place all the ingredients in a medium bowl and mix until smooth. Cover and refrigerate for at least 4 hours. The longer it refrigerates, the better the flavor will be.

Preheat a smoker or grill to 250°F.

To make the meat, trim the prime rib of any excess fat. Mix the mayonnaise and horseradish together in a small bowl, then smear over the prime rib. Next, add a liberal layer of the Operation BBQ Relief Texas SPG Rub and the Operation BBQ Relief Texas Santa Maria Steak Rub. Using a rasp grater, grate fresh horseradish root over the top of the prime rib.

Put the prime rib directly on the rack in the center of the smoker. Let it smoke for 1½ hours, then, using a meat thermometer, test the center section of the prime rib. Repeat this about every 20 minutes, or until an internal temperature of 125°F to 130°F is reached.

Remove the prime rib from the smoker and loosely tent it with foil. Let it rest for 15 to 20 minutes before carving. Slice the prime rib against the grain along the short side to desired thickness.

YIELD: 4 to 5 servings

BK'S JUICY JERKY
BRET AND KANDACE SABERHAGEN

Making your own homemade jerky is so simple! This beef jerky recipe calls for an overnight marinade and several hours in the smoker. While it takes time to make the perfect jerky, the hours of waiting will be worth it to snack on this flavorful meat!

BRINE

1 quart water

1 cup light brown sugar, unpacked

1 cup kosher salt

MEAT

1 (2 to 3-pound) full tri-tip

1 (16-ounce) bottle teriyaki sauce

To make the brine, place the water in a large bowl and add the brown sugar and salt. Mix well and refrigerate covered for 8 to 48 hours. Then add the tri-tip to the bowl and cover, allowing it to brine for 12 hours. Brining is a method used to add flavor to any meat product, as the meat will absorb the brine as it sits in the refrigerator.

Once the brining is complete, remove the meat from the brine using tongs and discard the brine. Set the meat on a large cutting board. Begin to slice the cut of meat, with the grain, into 3-inch-long and ½-inch-wide slices. Place the sliced meat into a large resealable plastic bag.

Pour the teriyaki sauce over the meat. Mix well and place in the refrigerator for 24 hours, massaging the bag periodically throughout the refrigeration process.

Preheat a smoker to 165°F. If there is a super-smoker option, use it. Place the meat on the racks and smoke for 3½ hours. Remove the meat from the racks when the jerky is very dark in color, has a very rigid texture, and is dry to the touch. Store in a resealable plastic bag.

YIELD: 8 to 10 servings

SKID BIRRIA
BRAD PENNY

Birria is a traditional Mexican dish from the state of Jalisco. This meat is prepared like a stew, and as a result, it is incredibly tender and flavorful. You can serve the birria as a stew, or you can take the meat and put it into tortillas for tacos!

SAUCE

4 dried ancho peppers

4 dried guajillo peppers

1 to 2 tablespoons fresh Vintage Farm almond oil

5 to 6 cups water

4 vine-ripe, medium-sized tomatoes, ½-inch diced

1 large white onion, ½-inch diced

20 peppercorns

6 whole cloves

3 teaspoons dried thyme

3 teaspoons marjoram

3 teaspoons Mexican oregano

5 to 6 bay leaves

1 cinnamon stick

10 cloves garlic

2 tablespoons salt

1½ teaspoons ground cumin

1½ teaspoons ground ginger

MEAT

3 pounds beef chuck roast

1 tablespoon Meat Church Holy VooDoo seasoning or your favorite seasoning

4 cups beef broth

To make the sauce, cut open and remove the stems and seeds from the dried peppers.

Place the oil in a medium frying pan and toast the peppers over medium-high heat, moving them continuously so they do not burn. Once toasted, remove the peppers from the pan and set them aside in a large bowl.

Boil the water and pour it over the peppers to rehydrate for 15 minutes. Reserve 4 cups of the water for later.

In the same frying pan, brown the tomatoes and onion in the reserved oil over medium heat for 5 to 10 minutes. Once browned, add all the other spices except for the cumin and ginger. Mix everything together well and cook for 5 to 10 minutes at medium to high heat. Remove the pan from the heat and let cool slightly.

Add the rehydrated peppers, tomato-onion mixture, cumin, and ginger to a blender. Once cool, add the reserved 4 cups of water used to rehydrate the peppers and blend until smooth. Set aside.

Preheat a smoker to 185°F.

Season the meat all over with your preferred seasoning and place it on the smoker for 2 hours.

Remove the meat and place it in a Dutch oven. Cover the meat with the prepared sauce and add the beef broth. Cover the pan.

Raise the heat of the smoker to 350°F. Place the Dutch oven in the smoker for 3 to 4 hours, checking the tenderness of the meat periodically. The internal temperature should reach around 205°F. Allow the meat to rest for 5 minutes before serving.

YIELD: 6 to 8 servings

Chapter 5

POULTRY

CHIPOTLE-SMOKED CHICKEN
ADRIANNA "AD" FRANCH

Nothing is better than a freshly smoked chicken. This recipe kicks up the flavor, adding the subtle smoky and spicy flavor of chipotle peppers with a hint of citrus. Be sure to make the chipotle butter ahead of time, so it can chill thoroughly before adding it under the skin of the chicken breast.

1 (3-pound) whole chicken

2 tablespoons Operation BBQ Relief Texas SPG Rub or your favorite rub

½ cup Chipotle Butter (page 158), divided

Place the chicken on a large cutting board, breast side down. Cut out the backbone of the chicken. Turn the chicken over, breast side up, and push down on the chicken breast to flatten.

Season the chicken with rub, on both the top and the bottom.

Place 1 tablespoon chipotle butter under the skin of each breast. Use the remaining chipotle butter to coat both the top and the bottom of the chicken.

Preheat a smoker to 250°F. Place the chicken in the smoker, skin side up. Smoke it for about 2 hours, or until it reaches an internal temperature of 165°F. Let it rest for 10 minutes before serving.

YIELD: 2 servings

SWEET 'N' SASSY BARBECUE SPATCHCOCKED CHICKEN

BRYAN MROCZKA

Removing the backbone of the chicken allows not only for quicker cooking but also for a more consistent product. You will enjoy the crispy skin paired with Sweet 'n' Sassy Barbecue Sauce. Make your own batch of the sauce ahead of time and add it right before the chicken is done in the smoker.

1 (3-pound) whole chicken

2 tablespoons butter, melted

2 tablespoons olive oil

1 tablespoon Operation BBQ Relief Sweet & Smoky Rub or your favorite rub

⅓ cup Operation BBQ Relief SPG Rub or your favorite rub

Sweet 'n' Sassy Barbecue Sauce (page 166)

Preheat a smoker to 375°F, adding your favorite wood.

Remove the backbone of the chicken using kitchen shears, then flatten the chicken out. Pound using a meat mallet. Inject the butter into the chicken.

Using a paper towel, dry the skin and inside of the chicken. Rub the oil over the skin and inside the chicken. Cover the skin side of the bird with the rubs.

Place the chicken in the smoker for about 45 minutes, or until the internal temperature reaches 160°F. Add the barbecue sauce to the skin side of the chicken and place it back in the smoker for about 10 minutes, or until the skin caramelizes.

Let the chicken rest for 5 minutes and serve.

YIELD: 4 servings

SPICY CHILI WINGS

EDDIE JACKSON

Eddie Jackson is amazing both on the football field and in the kitchen! He knows how to combine powerful flavors, and these chicken wings are just that. The hot sauce combined with the sweet chili sauce packs a punch on these wings.

SAUCE

2 cups sweet chili sauce

2 Thai chile peppers, stemmed

⅔ cups Louisiana hot sauce or your favorite hot sauce

8 tablespoons (1 stick) unsalted butter

1 tablespoon Cajun seasoning

WINGS

4 pounds chicken wings

6 tablespoons Cajun seasoning

6 tablespoons cornstarch

6 cups canola oil

2 green onions, thinly sliced

To make the sauce, place all the ingredients in a medium saucepan. Bring to a simmer over medium heat, just until the butter melts. Whisk to combine the butter into the sauce. Remove from the heat and reserve for the wings.

To make the wings, clean the chicken wings under cold water, then pat them dry with a paper towel. Ensure that the wings are completely dry.

In a large bowl, blend together the Cajun seasoning and cornstarch with a whisk, then add the wings. Toss until the wings are fully coated. Let the wings sit in the refrigerator, uncovered, at least 30 minutes before frying.

Fit a large pan with a drain rack.

Over medium heat, add the oil to a 7-quart Dutch oven or a proof pot with a lid. Use a fry/candy thermometer and bring the oil to 325°F. One at a time, add the wings to the hot oil. Cook them for 5 minutes, then move them to the large pan to drain.

Once all the wings have been through the first fry, increase the oil temperature to 375°F. One at a time, place the wings back in the oil to cook 5 to 6 minutes more, until the wings are golden brown.

Immediately after removing them from the hot oil, place the wings in a large bowl and toss them with the sauce. Top them with green onions and serve.

YIELD: 4 servings

SMOKY-SWEET GRILLED WINGS

ANDERS LEE

Growing up in Minnesota, Anders Lee learned the flavor of maple was a staple in a lot of cooking. This recipe combines the sweetness of maple with the spiciness of hot wings with just the right amount of smoke flavor.

BRINE

½ cup kosher salt

⅓ cup firmly packed light brown sugar

6 cups water

¼ cup apple cider

4 tablespoons maple syrup

WINGS

5 pounds chicken wings

5 tablespoons Operation BBQ Relief Sweet & Smoky Rub or your favorite rub

SAUCE

1 cup Frank's RedHot® cayenne pepper sauce or your favorite hot sauce

⅔ cup (1⅓ sticks) unsalted butter, melted

¼ cup maple syrup

2 tablespoons Operation BBQ Relief Cajun Bayou Rub or your favorite spicy rub

To make the brine, place the salt, brown sugar, and water in a bowl and mix to dissolve. Stir in the apple cider and maple syrup.

Place the chicken wings in a large, flat pan. Pour the brine over the chicken wings, making sure they are completely covered. Cover and place the chicken in the refrigerator to marinate for 12 hours.

After 12 hours, preheat a smoker to 250°F.

Remove the chicken wings from the brine and thoroughly rinse them with cold water. Discard the brine. Pat the chicken wings dry using a paper towel.

Coat the chicken wings with rub. Place the chicken wings on the smoker for 1½ hours, turning them halfway through.

While the wings are smoking, prepare the sauce. Place the hot sauce, butter, and maple syrup in a small saucepot. Warm over medium heat and stir until the sauce is hot and mixed well. Set aside.

Remove the chicken wings from the smoker and toss in a large bowl with the sauce until coated well.

Heat a grill to high. Place the wings on the grill and cook for 3 to 4 minutes more, until the internal temperature reaches 165°F. Continue to baste the wings with the remaining sauce.

Remove the wings from the grill and dust with rub. Line the chicken wings on a large platter and serve.

YIELD: 6 servings

BARBECUE STUFFED CHICKEN

BOB GOLIC

Chicken is one of the most popular items to cook out on the grill. This recipe combines the smoky flavor of hickory-smoked bacon with spicy pepper jack and finishes with a tangy-sweet barbecue sauce. Make sure to have some butcher's twine handy to keep the bacon, asparagus, and cheese all stuffed in the chicken while it is cooking!

1 medium-sized chicken breast

½ teaspoon Operation BBQ Relief Texas SPG Rub or your favorite rub, divided

4 slices ham

3 slices pepper jack cheese

3 to 4 blanched asparagus stalks

½ teaspoon Operation BBQ Relief Sweet & Smoky Rub or your favorite rub

Butcher's twine, for trussing

2 tablespoons canola oil

2 ounces chicken stock

SAUCE

¼ cup tangy barbecue sauce

¼ cup chicken stock

1 tablespoon apple cider vinegar

1 tablespoon apple butter

Trim any fat and cartilage that may be on the chicken breast. Place the chicken breast between 2 pieces of plastic wrap. Gently pound the chicken breast very thin using a meat mallet, about ¼ inch thick and about 6 inches wide by 8 inches long. Remove the top piece of plastic wrap.

Season the top of the chicken breast with ¼ teaspoon of the Operation BBQ Relief Texas SPG Rub. Cut the slices of ham to the width of the chicken breast and lay the ham side by side to cover the chicken.

Lay the cheese over the ham.

Trim the asparagus to about 6 inches long. Stack crosswise in the center of the chicken.

Starting from the bottom of the chicken, gently roll the chicken breast up to the top, keeping the ham and cheese inside, like a pinwheel. Tuck in the sides, similar to rolling a burrito.

Truss the chicken with butcher's twine to keep the chicken closed.

Season the stuffed chicken with the remaining ¼ teaspoon Operation BBQ Relief Texas SPG Rub and the Operation BBQ Relief Sweet & Smoky Rub.

Preheat a grill to 350°F. Place a large cast-iron skillet on the grill and add the oil. When hot, add the chicken and cook for a few minutes on each side, until all sides are brown.

Add the chicken stock, cover with aluminum foil, and move to a medium-heat side of the grill. Cook the chicken for about 20 minutes, or until the internal temperature reaches 165°F.

While the chicken is cooking, make the sauce. Combine all the ingredients in a small saucepot and slowly warm over low heat.

Remove the chicken from the grill and let rest for 2 minutes before slicing. Place the slices on a plate, drizzle with the sauce, and serve.

YIELD: 1 serving

SMOKED DUCK CONFIT PIZZA with ORANGE–PLUM SAUCE

JOHN RAILEY

Even though every kind of Chef Railey's pizza is delicious, this one knocks it out of the park. The combination of a fruity sauce and the decadent duck will leave you eating more and more slices.

DOUGH

1 (¼-ounce) packet dry instant yeast

1 teaspoon granulated sugar

1 cup warm water (about 70°F)

2½ cups bread flour, plus more for rolling

1 teaspoon salt

1 tablespoon canola oil

SAUCE

1 teaspoon olive oil

1 shallot, minced

6 red plums, pitted and cut into wedges

4 navel oranges, peeled and sliced into small sections

1 cup firmly packed light brown sugar

1 tablespoon apple cider

½ cup beef stock

¼ cup red wine (such as Cabernet)

DUCK

¼ cup olive oil, divided

6 to 8 (4-ounce) duck breasts, skin on

¼ cup Operation BBQ Relief Texas SPG Rub or your favorite seasoning

PIZZA

6 slices red onion (optional)

1 cup shredded mozzarella or provolone cheese blend

¼ cup arugula, for garnish

To make the dough, place the yeast, sugar, and water in a medium bowl and stir. Let the mixture sit for 15 minutes.

Stir in the flour, salt, and oil until blended. Let the mixture rest at room temperature for 10 minutes, then refrigerate, covered, for 45 minutes.

Remove the dough from the refrigerator and divide it to form two 8 to 10-ounce balls of dough. Keep the balls refrigerated until ready to use. Gently sprinkle flour on a surface and roll each piece of dough into a sphere about 4 inches wide.

To make the sauce, add the oil, shallot, plums, oranges, and brown sugar to a large saucepan. Cook over medium heat for approximately 5 minutes, stirring frequently, until the sugar dissolves and the plums have softened. Next, add the cider, stock, and wine. Let all the ingredients simmer for about 20 minutes, or until the sauce has thickened.

Remove the sauce from the heat and let it sit for 15 minutes, to thicken more, before serving.

Preheat a smoker to 300°F.

To make the duck, lightly drizzle 2 tablespoons of the oil over the breast, add the seasoning, and lay it flat, with the skin up, on a large baking sheet.

Place the baking sheet in the smoker and smoke the duck for about 2 hours, or until the meat is tender and has reached an internal temperature of 160°F.

Remove the baking sheet from the smoker, pull the skin off the duck, and lay the skin back on the baking sheet. Set the meat aside. Put the baking sheet back into the smoker for about 1 hour, or until the skin is crispy.

While the skin is cooking, drain the oil off the duck breast and shred it. Put the meat in a large pan, drizzle with 2 tablespoons of the olive oil, and place the pan back in the smoker for another hour, until the meat has reached 160°F.

Remove the duck from the smoker and let it sit for 15 minutes before serving. Take the pan with the skin out of the smoker and thinly slice the skin to make "duck cracklings" for a snack or garnish.

Preheat the oven to 500°F. Last, to make the pizza, roll out the dough on a peel lightly dusted with flour. Spread 4 ounces of the sauce over the top of each piece of dough, then sprinkle 3 tablespoons of the duck confit over the sauce, along with red onions, if using. Top each pizza with cheese, and sprinkle with duck cracklings.

Bake the pizzas in the oven for 7 to 8 minutes, until browned. If using an Ooni pizza oven, set it to 750°F and cook the pizzas for 3 to 4 minutes. Garnish with the arugula and serve.

YIELD: 8 servings

TURKEY BREAST ROULADE with JALAPEÑO CORN BREAD STUFFING

RAY "DR. BBQ" LAMPE

Turkey and corn bread are so great—why not combine them? A roulade is a flat piece of meat that is spread with a softer filling and rolled into a spiral. This dish looks fancy, but it is an easy way to combine unique flavors to make something delicious.

DRESSING

4 tablespoons (½ stick) unsalted butter

¼ cup finely chopped shallots

¼ cup finely chopped celery

1 medium jalapeño, seeded and finely chopped

¾ cup turkey or vegetable stock

1 tablespoon Dizzy Pig Mad Max Turkey Seasoning or your favorite seasoning

1½ cups dried corn bread stuffing mix

MEAT

1 (3-pound) boneless turkey breast

2 tablespoons olive oil

1 tablespoon Dizzy Pig Mad Max Turkey Seasoning or your favorite seasoning

4 ounces thinly sliced prosciutto

Butcher's twine, for tying the roast

Prepare a grill or smoker to cook in indirect heat at 300°F.

To make the dressing, place the butter in a medium saucepan over medium heat on the stove. When melted, add the shallot, celery, and jalapeño. Cook, stirring occasionally, for 4 to 5 minutes, until the shallots and celery are tender.

Add the stock and the seasoning, then stir. Bring to a full simmer. Add the stuffing mix and stir until well mixed. Set aside to cool while you prep the turkey breast.

To make the meat, remove the skin from the turkey breast and discard. Remove the tenderloin as well.

Lay the breast flat on a solid cutting board and cover it with plastic wrap. Using a heavy meat mallet, pound the breast to a thickness of about ½ inch, trying to shape it into a rectangle as you go.

Rub the turkey on both sides with a light coating of oil and a light dusting of seasoning.

Spread the dressing in an even layer on one side of the turkey, leaving a couple inches bare on one of the shorter edges. Starting with the opposite shorter edge, roll the turkey breast firmly but not too tight. Roll it so the final edge is facing down. Pull the roast to the edge closest to you.

Wrap the roast with prosciutto, making sure the prosciutto is overlapped slightly to ensure even coverage. The turkey should be completely covered by the prosciutto slices end to end.

Using about 10 pieces of butcher string, tie the roast about every 1½ inches, firmly but not too tight.

Brush the whole roast lightly with oil, then season it lightly with more of the seasoning. Transfer to the cooking grate and cook for 45 minutes to an hour, until the turkey reaches an internal temperature of 165°F.

Remove the turkey to a cutting board and let it rest for 5 minutes. Slice between the string, letting it hold everything together. Remove the string before serving.

YIELD: 4 servings

Operation BBQ Relief deploys numerous semi-trucks and tractor trailers with equipment, food, and supplies to provide tens of thousands of meals to communities impacted by disasters. The organization has over fifteen large commercial Ole Hickory Pit smokers stationed in areas around the country that can mobilize when needed. Together with other commercial kitchen equipment, Operation BBQ Relief could cook up to 60,000 hot fresh meals a day if needed. Operation BBQ Relief also has four smaller mobile trailers that are used to set up remote feeding locations away from the main food production area to help provide meals into communities.

Due to hotel shortages, volunteers, and staff that arrive from throughout the country bring their own recreational vehicles or have the option to utilize bunkhouses and showers provided by Operation BBQ Relief.

Chapter 6

BURGERS AND SANDWICHES

FRITO CUBANO

CARL RUIZ

A burger created by Carl Ruiz featuring the flavors of Cuba but, more importantly, it's a burger that he made because he always "did what he wanted"! #ruizing

1½ pounds 80/20 ground beef

½ pound ground Mexican chorizo, loose (if you can find only links, cut them open and remove the meat from the casings)

½ teaspoon kosher salt

½ teaspoon black pepper

12 slices Swiss cheese

12 mini King's Hawaiian rolls, halved

12 thin slices white onion

MOJO AIOLI

1 cup mayonnaise

2 tablespoons sour cream

2 teaspoons freshly grated lime zest

1 tablespoon freshly squeezed lime juice

1 tablespoon chopped fresh cilantro

1 clove garlic, minced

Pinch of kosher salt

Preheat a grill to high.

Place the ground beef, ground chorizo, salt, and pepper in a large bowl and mix. Divide the mixture and gently shape the meat into 12 equal-sized balls, then lightly press them into chubby round patties.

To make the aioli, whisk together all the ingredients in a small bowl. Cover and refrigerate until ready to assemble the burgers.

Grill the patties for 2 to 4 minutes, cooking until dark grill marks appear. Flip the burgers and cook for 2 to 4 minutes more, until the patties feel firm. Top each patty with a slice of cheese and cover with the lid to melt the cheese. Remove the patties from the grill and let them rest while you assemble the rest of the burgers.

Spread 1 tablespoon of the aioli on the bottom half of each roll, followed by a few slices of onion. Add a cooked burger to each, then the top half of a bun. Serve.

YIELD: 6 servings

SMOKED PORK LOIN SANDWICH
JOHNNY IMBRIOLO

Smoked pork loin is the perfect meat to make for family dinner or for your next backyard barbecue! Adding the yellow mustard packs in the flavor, provides moistness to the meat, and allows the rub to stick to something. Use your favorite rub to make this dish your own!

1 (4 to 6-pound) whole pork loin

3 tablespoons yellow mustard

3 tablespoons Operation BBQ Relief Sweet & Smoky Rub or your favorite rub

6 to 8 sandwich buns

1½ to 2 cups barbecue sauce, divided

Preheat a smoker to 250°F.

Coat the entire pork loin with mustard and sprinkle the rub over the entire pork loin.

Place the pork loin in the smoker and cook for 4 hours, or until golden brown and the internal temperature has reached 140°F.

Remove the pork from the smoker and allow it to rest before slicing. The pork will continue to rise in temperature to 145°F.

Shave the pork into very thin slices and place on the bottom bun. Top with about ¼ cup barbecue sauce and finish with the top bun. Repeat for additional sandwiches.

YIELD: 6 to 8 servings

SMOKED BARBECUE REUBEN

MIKE GOLIC

This is a creative twist that combines the best of a classic Reuben and backyard barbecue all-in-one sandwich! By spreading butter on the bread, it ensures a nice toast. Once you get the golden brown on the bread, transferring it to the oven allows the cheese to melt without the bread getting burned.

2 thick slices seedless rye bread

1 tablespoon Thousand Island dressing

1 tablespoon your favorite barbecue sauce

4 slices Swiss cheese

6 ounces thinly shaved smoked pork loin

¼ teaspoon barbecue spice

1 ounce prepared coleslaw

5 thinly sliced pickle rounds

2 tablespoons unsalted butter, softened

Preheat an oven to 350°F. Lay both slices of bread on a cutting board.

Place the dressing and barbecue sauce in a small bowl and mix to combine. Spread over each slice of bread.

Place two slices of cheese on one side of the bread. Place the pork loin evenly on top of the cheese and sprinkle with barbecue spice.

Evenly place the coleslaw on top of the pork. Place the pickle slices on top of the coleslaw, then place the last two slices of cheese on top of the pickles.

Place the remaining slice of bread on top to complete the sandwich.

Preheat a nonstick sauté pan over medium heat. Evenly butter both sides of the sandwich and place into the pan. Cook for about 2 minutes on each side, or until the bread is golden brown.

Remove the sandwich from the pan and place it on a cookie sheet. Finish cooking it in the oven for 4 to 5 minutes. When the sandwich is hot and the cheese is melted, remove it from the oven. Cut the sandwich in half and serve.

YIELD: 1 serving

GRILLED LAMB SANDWICHES
with HARISSA MAYO

There is nothing better than these tender pieces of lamb sandwiched between a sourdough baguette. Topped with a slightly spicy mayo, this sandwich packs a ton of flavor.

HARISSA MAYONNAISE

½ cup real mayonnaise

¼ cup sour cream

2 tablespoons harissa paste

½ teaspoon red wine vinegar

¼ teaspoon ground cumin

Salt and freshly ground black pepper

MARINADE

½ tablespoon capers, rinsed

1 teaspoon fresh oregano leaves

4 cloves garlic

2 cups plain, unsweetened yogurt

2 tablespoons olive oil

½ teaspoon freshly grated lemon zest

2 teaspoons kosher salt

1 teaspoon black pepper

MEAT

1 (3 to 4-pound) leg of lamb

2 teaspoons olive oil

TOPPINGS

1 hothouse cucumber, thinly sliced

1 Fresno chile, halved, seeded, and sliced thin

1 cup white vinegar

¾ cup sugar

½ cup water

1 teaspoon kosher salt

1 sourdough baguette

To make the harissa mayonnaise, place all the ingredients in a large bowl and whisk to combine. Season with salt and pepper to taste. Cover and refrigerate until ready to use.

To make the marinade, finely mince the capers, oregano, and garlic together. Transfer to a small bowl along with the yogurt, olive oil, lemon zest, salt, and pepper, stirring until well combined.

Place the lamb in a resealable plastic bag and pour in the marinade. Mix it around so the lamb is completely coated. Squeeze out any air, reseal the bag, and place it in the refrigerator for at least 30 minutes or up to overnight.

Preheat a grill to medium-high heat.

Continued

When the lamb is done marinating, remove it from the bag and wipe off any excess marinade with paper towels. Discard the marinade. Unfold the lamb, drizzle with oil, and sprinkle well with salt and pepper on both sides. This will help form a nice crust.

Grill for about 15 minutes, then flip once. Cook for another 12 minutes on the second side, or until cooked through to an internal temperature of 145°F and there is some color on the lamb. When done, remove it from the grill, tent with foil, and let rest for 10 to 12 minutes before carving across the grain into thin slices.

To prepare the toppings, add the cucumber and chiles to a medium bowl and toss to combine. In a medium saucepan, add the vinegar, sugar, water, and salt. Heat gently, stirring, just until the sugar and salt dissolve. Pour over the cucumbers and chiles in the bowl. Set aside to marinate for at least 15 minutes before serving.

Cut the baguette in half lengthwise, horizontally. Place the bread on the grill for about 2 minutes per side, or until warm and slightly crisp.

To assemble the sandwiches, smear the bottom of the bread with harissa mayo and stack with slices of lamb. Drain the cucumbers and chiles, and discard the liquid. Place the cucumbers and chiles on top of the lamb, followed by the top of the baguette. Slice the sandwich into quarters and serve.

YIELD: 4 servings

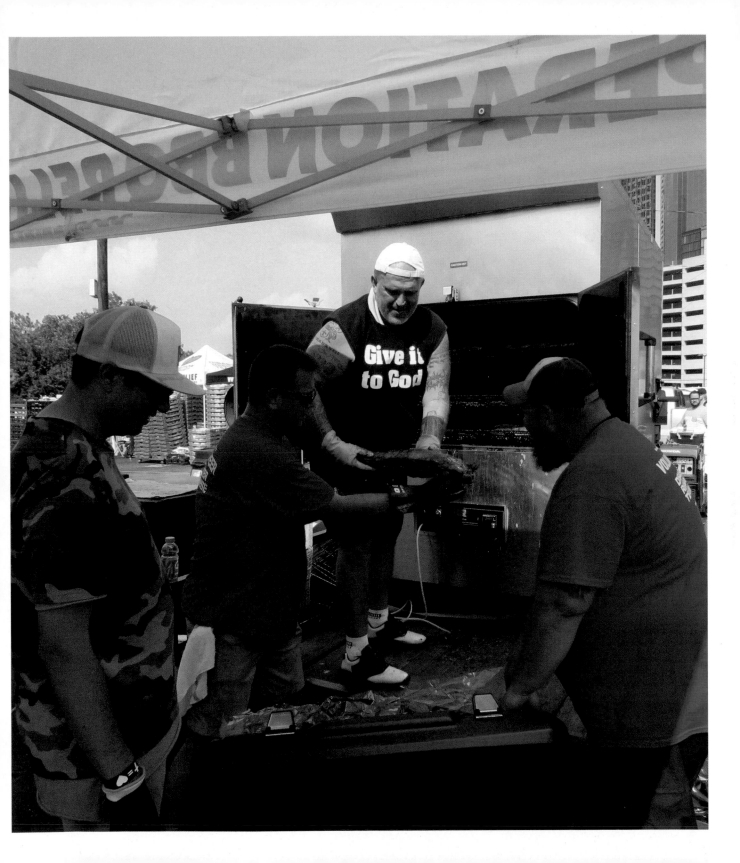

ONION SMASH BURGER

TOM BURGMEIER

This burger is packed with classic flavor. The grilled sweet onions, melty cheese, crisp smoky bacon, and pickles all make this burger fantastic. Make sure you have some napkins handy because the melted cheese and juicy burger will be bursting out of the bun!

12 ounces 80/20 ground beef

1 teaspoon canola oil

1 small Vidalia onion, finely shredded using a grater or food processor

1 teaspoon Operation BBQ Relief Texas SPG Rub or your favorite rub, divided

2 slices American cheese

1 King's Hawaiian roll or your favorite burger bun

4 slices thick-cut hickory-smoked bacon, cooked

4 thick-cut pickle slices

Divide the ground beef into two 6-ounce balls.

Coat a hot griddle with the oil over high heat.

Place the burger meat on the hot griddle and, using a spatula, smash the burgers so they are approximately ¼ inch thick. Cover each burger with onions and smash them down with the spatula. Sprinkle the top of the onions with half of the rub.

Cook for 1½ minutes, then flip the burgers over. Season the bottom of the burgers with the remaining rub. Cook for 1 minute more. The burgers should reach an internal temperature of 165°F. Place a slice of cheese on each burger and cover so the cheese will melt.

Toast the buns on the griddle for 1 to 2 minutes, until lightly brown.

Remove the bottom bun and place it on a cutting board. Top with one of the burgers. Add two slices of bacon, then top with the second burger. Top with the remaining two slices of bacon. Place the pickle slices on top of the second burger and finish with the top bun.

YIELD: 1 serving

CHICKEN SHAWARMA SANDWICH

STAN HAYS

This chicken sandwich is the perfect food to make ahead of time for quick and easy dinner! By marinating the chicken overnight and preparing the sauce the night before, you allow all the spices to soak into the dish. The next day, all you have to do is fire up the grill, and dinner is served!

MARINADE

1 tablespoon minced garlic
(2 cloves)

1 tablespoon ground coriander

1 tablespoon ground cumin

1 tablespoon ground cardamom

1 tablespoon ground turmeric

½ teaspoon onion powder

1 tablespoon smoked paprika

1 teaspoon ground cayenne pepper

1 teaspoon kosher salt

½ teaspoon black pepper

Juice from ½ medium lemon

2 tablespoons plain Greek yogurt

3 tablespoons olive oil

2 pounds boneless, skinless
chicken thighs

YOGURT SAUCE

1 cup plain Greek yogurt

1 clove garlic, grated

1 teaspoon ground cumin

Juice from ½ medium lemon

1 teaspoon salt

1 teaspoon black pepper

SANDWICHES

4 flatbreads (naan, pita bread, or
regular bun)

1 cup diced tomatoes

2 cups shredded lettuce

For the marinade, place all the ingredients in a resealable plastic bag and add the chicken thighs. Make sure all the thighs are coated with the marinade. Marinate overnight for best results.

To make the yogurt sauce, combine the ingredients in a small bowl and chill. Refrigerate covered overnight for best results.

Preheat a grill to high heat, about 400°F, to get some char on the chicken. Remove the chicken from the marinade and discard the remaining marinade. Grill the chicken for 6-8 minutes until the internal temperature is 160°F. Remove the chicken from the grill, cover it with foil, and let it rest for 5 minutes. Slice the chicken thighs very thin, about the thickness of pencils.

To make the sandwiches, start with a piece of the flatbread, spoon on some yogurt sauce, and pile the chicken on top, then some lettuce and tomato—and don't forget to add a little more yogurt sauce on top! You can enjoy this with Mediterranean yellow rice or a salad.

YIELD: 4 sandwiches

TEXAS PATTY MELT

JOHNNY IMBRIOLO

You have all heard of a patty melt, but this puts a barbecue twist on it. Brisket burnt ends are the flavorful, fattier parts of a brisket that are a staple of Kansas City barbecue. Putting these on a sandwich ensures bold flavors that are packed between two buttery pieces of Texas toast.

2 slices Texas toast

4 slices American cheese

6 ounces brisket burnt ends, hot

1 ounce tangy barbecue sauce

1 ounce chopped grilled onion, hot

4 slices pickled jalapeños

2 tablespoons unsalted butter, softened

Place the Texas toast on a platter, then place two slices of American cheese on each slice of bread.

Place the burnt ends on one side of the bread, then drizzle the barbecue sauce and pile the onions on top.

Place the jalapeños on top of the onions and top with the remaining slice of bread. Butter both sides of the sandwich and place it in a nonstick pan over medium heat.

Toast the sandwich for about 2 minutes on each side, or until the bread is golden brown and the cheese is melted. Remove the sandwich from the pan, cut in half, and enjoy.

YIELD: 1 serving

SMOKED CHICKEN & PEAR QUESADILLA
BRYAN MROCZKA

This recipe is great as an appetizer or as a meal! Brie is known for its creaminess, which makes it a perfect melting cheese for this quesadilla. Brie also pairs well with fruits, which is why combining it with pear works so perfectly.

2 (10-inch) flour tortillas

2 tablespoons bacon jam

8 (¼-inch-thick) slices Brie

½ teaspoon barbecue spice

6 ounces chopped hickory-smoked chicken (white and dark meat combined)

¼ ripe Anjou pear

2 teaspoons sliced green onions

Cooking spray

Place the tortillas on a cutting board and spread 1 tablespoon of the jam on each evenly, leaving a ¼-inch rim around the edge.

Place 4 slices of Brie on top of each tortilla, spacing evenly.

Sprinkle barbecue spice over the cheese.

Spread the chicken evenly over one of the tortillas.

Remove the skin and the seeds from the pear and slice very thin. Place the pear slices on top of the chicken, spreading them evenly.

Sprinkle the green onions over the pear. Take the remaining tortilla, with jam and Brie, and place it on top of the other tortilla.

Heat a nonstick pan over medium-high heat. Spray the pan with cooking spray and, when it is heated, place the quesadilla into the pan.

Cook for about 2 to 3 minutes on each side, using a spatula to turn the quesadilla.

When both sides are crispy and brown and the cheese inside has melted, remove the quesadilla from the pan and cut it into equal triangles.

YIELD: 1 serving

Chapter 7
SEAFOOD

CEDAR PLANK SOY–HONEY SALMON

Spicing up a classical regional dish, this salmon is cooked on a cedar plank. A cedar plank helps prevent the fish from charring on the grill, but still gives it a signature smoky flavor! Pairing the smoky flavor with sweet honey of the glaze, makes this the perfect dish.

2 cedar planks

5 pounds salmon, with skin on

1 tablespoon Operation BBQ Relief Cajun Bayou Rub or your favorite rub

1 tablespoon Operation BBQ Relief Florida Mojo Rub or your favorite rub

GLAZE

⅔ cup honey

⅓ cup soy sauce

First, soak the cedar planks in water for a couple hours before starting the salmon.

Preheat a grill to 225°F.

Pat the salmon dry and cut it in half crosswise. Rub one half of the non-skin side of the salmon with the Cajun rub and the other non-skin half with the Florida Mojo rub.

Place each half of the salmon on a cedar plank, skin side down, and add the cedar planks to the grill. Cook for 20 minutes.

While the salmon is cooking, make the glaze. Mix the honey and soy sauce in a small saucepan. Cook over medium heat until well combined and reduce by about one-third. Pour in a squirt bottle and let cool.

Remove the planks with the salmon when it reaches 145°F, after about 20 minutes. While the salmon is hot, squirt some of the glaze over the salmon and remove it from the cedar planks. Make sure you serve each guest a piece from the two different halves so they can enjoy the different flavors of each rub.

YIELD: 6 servings

CAMPENCHANA

KATHY RUIZ

Campenchana is a great Texas/Gulf of Mexico dish that would really complement barbecue items. This recipe was developed on the Gulf Coast using fresh gulf shrimp and blue crab meat. It is spicy, refreshing, and delicious!

2 poblano peppers

½ pound 21/25 count shrimp

¾ teaspoon kosher salt, divided

1 small tomato, finely chopped

2 jalapeños, seeded and finely chopped

½ cup Clamato juice

¼ cup ketchup

3 tablespoons chopped fresh cilantro, plus leaves for garnish

2 tablespoons finely chopped white onion

½ teaspoon finely chopped garlic

3 tablespoons freshly squeezed lime juice

3 tablespoons olive oil

½ pound jumbo lump crabmeat, picked through for shells

1 avocado, pitted, peeled, and ¼-inch diced

Tortilla chips, for serving

Preheat a grill to high heat. Place the peppers directly over the flame, turning occasionally, and grill for 10 to 12 minutes, until very tender and blackened all over.

Transfer the peppers to a medium bowl. Cover the bowl with plastic wrap and let the peppers steam for 15 minutes. Peel the peppers and discard the seeds. Dice into ¼-inch pieces.

Meanwhile, add ½ teaspoon of the salt to a medium pot of water and bring to a boil. Cook the shrimp for 2 to 3 minutes, until just opaque and pink. Using a slotted spoon, transfer the shrimp to an ice bath and let them sit until cool, about 3 minutes, then drain, peel, devein, and remove the tails. Set aside.

Mix the poblanos, tomato, jalapeño, Clamato, ketchup, cilantro, onion, garlic, lime juice, oil, and the remaining ¼ teaspoon salt in a large bowl. Carefully fold in the shrimp, crab, and avocado.

Transfer to a large serving vessel. Garnish with a few cilantro leaves and serve with tortilla chips.

YIELD: 3 to 4 servings

SHRIMP and CRISPY GRITS
CLARENCE CEASAR

If you've eaten in the South, no doubt you have tried shrimp and grits. This dish, infused with the aroma of peppers to produce tender, spicy shrimp and crispy sweet corn grits is a meal that can be enjoyed any time of the day.

GRITS

1 cup water

1 teaspoon unsalted butter

⅛ teaspoon kosher salt

¼ cup instant grits

1 teaspoon canola oil

½ cup panko bread crumbs

SHRIMP

1 tablespoon canola oil

6 (16/20 count) shrimp, peeled, tails left on

¼ teaspoon Operation BBQ Relief Cajun Bayou Rub or your favorite rub

¼ teaspoon chopped garlic

¼ cup sliced yellow onion

¼ cup sliced red pepper

¼ cup sliced green pepper

¼ teaspoon kosher salt

2 tablespoons white wine

4 tablespoons tomato sauce

2 tablespoons water

¼ teaspoon ground chipotle pepper

1 teaspoon sliced green onions

To make the grits, place the water, butter, and salt in a medium saucepot and bring to a boil over high heat. Slowly stir in the grits and continue to stir until the grits are well blended.

Lower the heat to a simmer and continue to stir until the grits start to thicken. Pour the grits into a pie tin and place in the refrigerator. Let cool until the grits are firm.

In the meantime, put the breadcrumbs in a food processor and pulse for 30 seconds until fine. Once the grits are firm, heat a large, nonstick skillet over medium heat and add the oil.

Remove the grits from the pie tin and sprinkle both sides of the grit cake with the bread crumbs. Place in the pan to crisp the grit cake. Cook for 2 minutes, then flip to crisp for 2 minutes more. Remove from the heat but leave the cake in the pan.

To make the shrimp, heat a medium sauté pan over medium heat and add the oil.

Season the shrimp with rub and place the shrimp into the pan of hot oil. Cook the shrimp for 1 minute, then turn and add the garlic, onions, and peppers. Sauté for 1 minute more.

Add the salt, wine, tomato sauce, water, and ground chipotle pepper to the pan with the shrimp. Lower the heat to a simmer and cook for 2 minutes.

Remove the crispy grit cake from the other pan and place in the center of a plate. Place the peppers and onions in a pile on top of the grit cake. Arrange the shrimp on top of the peppers and onions. Pour the sauce over the shrimp and around the grit cake. Sprinkle with the green onions and serve.

YIELD: 1 serving

BARBECUE SHRIMP
BRET AND KANDACE SABERHAGEN

This recipe is so simple, yet so delicious. By using spices and ingredients you already have in the pantry, this meal can be whipped up in no time. Barbecue shrimp are perfect served with Bacon-Wrapped Asparagus (page 34) or some rich and creamy Mac 'n Cheese (page 37).

1 tablespoon smoked paprika

1 tablespoon chili powder

1 tablespoon brown sugar

1 teaspoon sea salt

½ teaspoon black pepper

½ teaspoon ground cumin

1 tablespoon minced garlic

1 tablespoon olive oil

½ lemon

2 pounds 16/20 count shrimp, peeled and deveined

6 thinly sliced green onions

Preheat a grill to medium heat.

Place all the ingredients, except for the lemon, shrimp, and green onions, in a large bowl and mix well.

Squeeze the lemon over the shrimp. Add the shrimp and green onions to the bowl and toss to coat. Refrigerate for 10 minutes.

Grill the shrimp for 2 minutes on each side, until slightly pink. These are great by themselves or even in tacos.

YIELD: 6 servings

TC BARBECUE SHRIMP DISH

Nothing is better than a plate of buttery shrimp! Five sticks of butter may seem like a lot, but the rich flavors are unmatched. Slice up your favorite kind of bread, and it will readily absorb the rich lemon-garlic flavors of the shrimp and the butter sauce.

2½ cups (5 sticks) unsalted butter

½ sweet onion, sliced ⅛ inch thick

1 clove chopped garlic

3 lemons, sliced ⅛ inch thick

½ cup Chef Paul Prudhomme Blackened Redfish Magic Seasoning or your favorite seasoning

2 pounds 16/20 count shrimp, peeled, tails left on

1 baguette, sliced thin, for serving

Melt the butter in a large skillet or wok over medium heat.

Place the onions, garlic, lemons, and seasoning in the pan and cook for 2 minutes.

When everything is broken down and soft, add the shrimp and simmer for 2 to 3 minutes, then turn off the heat to let rest. Pour onto a large serving platter and serve with lots of sliced bread.

YIELD: 8 servings

SALMON TACOS with CILANTRO-LIME SLAW and MANGO SALSA

DEWAYNE DANIEL

A great fish taco is always refreshing! The cilantro-lime slaw and the mango salsa add bold flavors while still keeping the taco light and fresh.

CILANTRO-LIME SLAW

½ cup real mayonnaise

2 teaspoons apple cider vinegar

1 teaspoon sugar

Juice from 1 lime

2 cups finely shredded green cabbage

¼ cup chopped fresh cilantro

Salt and freshly ground black pepper

MANGO SALSA

1 ripe mango, peeled and cut into ¼-inch dice

1 small shallot, chopped

1 chile pepper, seeded and chopped finely (depending on the heat level desired: poblano for mild, jalapeño for hot, serrano for even hotter)

Juice from 1 lime

Salt and freshly ground black pepper

TACOS

2 (4 to 5-ounce) salmon fillets, skin on

1 teaspoon grapeseed oil, for the salmon skin

1 teaspoon grapeseed oil, for the skillet

Citrus Rub (page 162), Operation BBQ Relief Florida Mojo Rub, or your favorite rub

6 corn tortillas

To make the slaw, place the mayonnaise, vinegar, sugar, and lime juice in a medium bowl and whisk. Add the cabbage and cilantro and toss until completely coated. Season with salt and pepper to taste. Refrigerate until ready to serve.

To make the mango salsa, mix the mango, shallot, chile pepper, and lime juice in a medium bowl. Season with salt and pepper to taste. Refrigerate until ready to serve.

Rub the salmon fillets with oil. Apply a generous amount of rub on the non-skin side only.

Preheat a grill to 400°F to 450°F. Place a medium-sized griddle or a cast-iron skillet on the grill and apply a medium amount of oil.

Place the salmon fillets on the griddle, skin side down, and cook for 6 to 8 minutes. The fish will be ready to flip when it releases naturally from the griddle. Flip the salmon and cook for 1 to 2 minutes more for doneness and color. Remove from the grill.

Place the tortillas on the grill for 1 minute to gently warm. Assemble each taco with a few pieces of salmon, a spoonful of slaw, and a spoonful of mango salsa. Enjoy!

YIELD: 2 servings

GRILLED GINGER and SOY TUNA STEAK

JOHNNY IMBRIOLO

This restaurant-quality recipe is the perfect blend of Asian and Southwest flavors. Decorated with bright colors and mashed avocados, the amazing flavors are perfect for a light lunch on a hot summer day. Make sure to prepare the vegetables the night before for the most robust flavors.

PICKLED VEGETABLES

½ medium red onion, sliced into ⅛-inch-thick matchstick slices

1 jalapeño, seeded and sliced into ¹⁄₁₆-inch-thick slices

2 cloves garlic, smashed

½ cup red wine vinegar

½ cup apple cider vinegar

1 cup water

¼ cup honey

½ teaspoon kosher salt

TUNA

2 (8-ounce) Ahi tuna steaks, sushi grade

3 tablespoons low-sodium soy sauce

1-inch piece fresh ginger, peeled and grated

1 teaspoon kosher salt

Canola oil, for oiling the grill

2 avocados, pitted and peeled

2 tablespoons chopped fresh cilantro, plus additional leaves for garnish

2 lime wedges, for garnish

To make the pickled vegetables, place the red onion, jalapeño, and garlic in a medium bowl.

In a medium saucepan, add the vinegars, water, honey, and salt. Bring to a boil over medium-high heat, then remove from the heat.

Allow the liquid to cool slightly. Add the onions, jalapeños, and garlic, cover, and marinate overnight.

After 24 hours, remove the onions, jalapeños, and garlic from the marinade and set aside the vegetables. Discard the marinade.

To make the tuna, place the tuna steaks in a resealable plastic bag and add the soy sauce and ginger, rubbing into the tuna. Seal the bag tightly and place in the refrigerator for 1 hour.

Preheat a grill to 325°F, then oil it well with the canola oil. Remove the tuna steaks from the bag and brush off any soy and ginger. Discard remaining marinade.

Season the tuna with ½ teaspoon of the kosher salt on each side and place it on the grill. Cook the tuna steaks for 1½ minutes on each side.

While the tuna is cooking, place the avocado in a medium bowl and add the remaining ½ teaspoon kosher salt and the cilantro. Mash the avocado and mix well.

Place the avocado in a line down the center of a serving plate.

Remove the tuna from the grill and place it on a cutting board, allowing it to rest for 1 minute. Slice the tuna steak into ¼-inch-thick slices and shingle them on top of the avocado.

Sprinkle the pickled onion and jalapeño down the center of the tuna steak. Garnish with fresh cilantro leaves and lime wedges.

YIELD: 2 servings

SEAFOOD "BOIL" with CAJUN BUTTER

DAVID ROSE

Many people have had a traditional seafood boil, but have you ever had a smoked seafood boil? Perfectly charred lobster tails, shrimp, corn and potatoes fresh off the smoky grill, slathered in Cajun butter.

Smoke this tasty treat up any time of the year, and instantly transport your taste buds to the coast!

SEAFOOD SEASONING

½ cup kosher salt

2 teaspoons black pepper

2 teaspoons smoked paprika

2 teaspoons garlic powder

2 teaspoons onion powder

1 teaspoon celery seed

¼ teaspoon cayenne pepper

CAJUN GARLIC BUTTER

2 tablespoons olive oil

1 minced whole shallot

3 cloves garlic, minced

1 pound (4 sticks) unsalted butter

1 tablespoon freshly grated lemon zest

½ teaspoon smoked paprika

¼ teaspoon cayenne pepper

½ teaspoon dried thyme leaves

½ teaspoon onion powder

½ teaspoon black pepper

½ teaspoon kosher salt

2 tablespoons chopped fresh Italian parsley

SMOKED SEAFOOD "BOIL"

1 pound petite red potatoes (8 to 10 potatoes)

4 ears sweet yellow corn, shucked and halved crosswise

4 lobster tails, halved lengthwise

1 pound 12/16 count jumbo shrimp, peeled and deveined

1 pound kielbasa sausage (4 to 5 sausage links)

½ cup olive oil

8 to 10 wooden skewers, soaked for 2 hours in 1 cup water

1 cup cherrywood or applewood chips, soaked for 2 hours in 1 cup water

Canola oil, for oiling the grill

1 loaf French bread, sliced into 4 equal parts

2 whole lemons, halved, for serving

Prepare a grill to medium-high heat, between 450°F and 500°F. To make the seafood seasoning, place all the ingredients in a small bowl and whisk to combine. Set aside.

On the stovetop, fill a medium saucepan with water, add a heavy pinch of salt, and set to high heat. Once the water is boiling, add the potatoes and cook for 10 to 12 minutes, until fork tender. Remove the potatoes from the water and cool to room temperature.

Meanwhile, to make the garlic butter, place a medium heavy-duty or cast-iron saucepot directly on the grill and add the oil. Add the shallots and garlic to the saucepot and sauté for 20 to 30 seconds, until fragrant but not browned. Add the butter, lemon zest, seasonings, and parsley and whisk for 1 to 2 minutes, until all the ingredients are incorporated. Once the butter is fully melted, immediately remove the pot from the heat and set aside.

Once the potatoes are cool, slice them in half and place them on a large sheet pan, along with the corn and lobster tails. Double-skewer the shrimp and lay the skewers on the same sheet pan. Drizzle the shrimp skewers, lobster, potatoes, and corn with oil and season liberally with the seafood seasoning. Toss until all ingredients are well coated.

Add the wood chips on top of the hot coals in the grill and oil the grill grates with oil on a paper towel to prevent sticking. Place the shrimp skewers, corn, lemon halves meat side down, kielbasa meat side down, potatoes meat side down, and lobster tails meat side down on the grill and cook for 4 to 5 minutes.

Once nicely charred, remove the lemons from the grill and set aside. Flip the shrimp skewers, corn, kielbasa, potatoes, and lobster tails and continue to grill for another 4 to 5 minutes, until cooked through and golden brown.

Line a large sheet pan with newspaper or pink butcher paper. Remove all the ingredients from the grill and transfer to the sheet pan. Remove the shrimp from the skewers and arrange all the grilled ingredients on top of the paper.

Meanwhile, brush each section of the bread on both sides with the garlic butter. Grill the bread face down for 40 to 50 seconds, until crispy and slightly charred. Once finished, remove the bread from the grill and slice it into about 16 servings.

Arrange the shrimp, corn, kielbasa, potatoes, and lobster tails on a sheet pan and baste liberally with garlic butter on both sides. Drizzle the remaining garlic butter on top and serve with toasted bread and lemon halves. Enjoy!

YIELD: 16 servings

GRILLED MAHI-MAHI TOSTADA

JUSTIN MORROW

A tostada is like a taco, but flat. This hard tortilla base may not be the easiest meal to eat but is sure delicious. All the bright, fresh flavors of this dish are the perfect accompaniment to the grilled mahi-mahi. This is the perfect light lunch on a warm summer day.

½ medium red onion, thinly sliced

1 jalapeño, seeded and thinly sliced

1 cup water

1 cup apple cider vinegar

4 tablespoons honey

1 teaspoon kosher salt

2 (5-ounce) mahi-mahi fillets

1 teaspoon canola oil

2 teaspoons Operation BBQ Relief Florida Mojo Rub or your favorite rub

1 avocado, pitted and peeled

2 tostadas

¼ teaspoon kosher salt

2 springs cilantro, leaves stripped

½ fresh lime

Place the red onion and jalapeño in a medium bowl. Add the water, vinegar, honey, and salt. Mix to combine. Cover and refrigerate overnight.

Preheat a grill to 325°F. Coat the mahi-mahi fillets with oil and season both sides with the rub. Place the fillets on the grill and cook for 2 minutes on each side, or until golden brown.

While the mahi-mahi is grilling, smash the avocado in a small bowl. Divide the avocado between the tostadas, leaving a ¼-inch rim around the edge. Sprinkle the avocado with salt.

To assemble, place the cooked mahi-mahi on top of the avocado. Remove the pickled onions and jalapeño from the refrigerator, drain, and discard the remaining marinade. Add the pickled vegetables to the top of the fish. Place a few cilantro leaves on top of the onions. Squeeze fresh lime juice over the top and serve.

YIELD: 2 servings

SMOKED WALLEYE SALAD
with ARTICHOKES
COLBY GARRELTS

Walleye is a freshwater fish whose texture can be described as buttery. This delicate, flakey fish from North America is the perfect fish to smoke. Smoked walleye pairs well with cooked artichokes.

SMOKED WALLEYE

4½ cups water

4½ tablespoons kosher salt

3½ tablespoons white sugar

Finely grated zest of one medium lemon

Finely grated zest of one medium lime

1 tablespoons toasted, crushed coriander

2 teaspoons toasted, crushed celery seed

2 pounds walleye

ARTICHOKES

3 quarts water

1 medium lemon

4 medium artichokes

½ cup olive oil

2 cups white wine

1 small shallot, minced

8 cloves garlic

1 tablespoon dried oregano

1 tablespoon dried thyme

1 teaspoon kosher salt

1 teaspoon black pepper

To make the brine for the walleye, whisk all of the ingredients together in a large bowl. Place the walleye and the brine in a sealed, airtight container and leave in the fridge for 12 hours.

Preheat a smoker to 200°F. Remove the fish from the brine and discard. Smoke the fish over low heat for 2 hours. The fish is done smoking when it reaches an internal temperature of 160°F and easily flakes with a fork.

For the artichokes, pour the water in a large bowl. Cut the lemon in half and mix the juice with the water.

Prepare the artichokes by removing the stems, tough outer leaves, and tips from the artichokes. Quarter the artichokes and cut out the choke. The choke has a red tip and is very tough, and there are thin fibers on the base of the choke; both should be removed. Using a teaspoon, carefully insert the spoon under the red leaves and, grasping the choke with your thumb, pull the choke toward the base until it rips free. Continue until all red pieces and thin fibers are removed. Cut them into ½ inch wedges and place in the lemon water to keep them from oxidizing.

In a medium saucepan over medium heat, add the olive oil and white wine. Bring to a very low simmer.

Drain the artichokes from the lemon water and add to the saucepan with the shallots, garlic, herbs, salt, and pepper. Cover the pot and braise the artichokes until they are fork tender, about 45 minutes.

Remove from the heat. Add the artichokes and all the cooking liquid to a fresh container and chill in the refrigerator until completely chilled, about 2 hours.

Once chilled, remove the artichokes from the cooking liquid and arrange on a large platter with the smoked walleye for a light, refreshing summer salad.

YIELD: 4 servings

Chapter 8

DESSERTS

MY MOTHER'S RUM CAKE

Because this recipe has a strong amount of rum, it's for adults only. This makes a "double batch" of frosting, so cut the amount of frosting in half for a less intoxicating version. The cake is best served after sitting overnight to let the flavors soak in, so plan ahead!

CAKE

1 (15.25-ounce) box yellow cake mix

4 large eggs

½ cup canola oil

½ cup golden rum

FROSTING

1 cup golden rum

2 cups sugar

1 cup (2 sticks) unsalted butter

Preheat an oven to 350°F. Grease a Bundt pan.

To make the cake, place the cake mix, eggs, oil, and rum in a large bowl and mix with an electric mixer for about 3 minutes, or until smooth. Pour into the prepared Bundt pan and place in the oven.

While the cake is baking, make the frosting. On a stovetop over medium heat, mix the rum, sugar, and butter in a medium saucepan until it boils. Decrease the heat and simmer for 10 to 15 minutes, stirring often.

Once the cake has baked for 45 to 50 minutes, check for doneness by inserting a toothpick. It is done when the toothpick comes out clean. Turn the warm cake over onto a large plate. Poke holes in the cake with a knife or fork and pour the frosting over it. Cover the cake and let it sit overnight so the frosting can soak in before serving.

YIELD: 8 servings

STRABERRY COBBLER

ALAN NICHOLS

Nothing says "summer" more than strawberries, and using freshly picked strawberries in this cobbler amps up this already delicious dessert. Topped with a scoop of vanilla ice cream, this cobbler will melt in your mouth.

TOPPING

4 to 6 cups strawberries, washed, hulled, and sliced ¼ inch thick

2 cups water

¾ cup sugar

½ cup cold water

3 tablespoons cornstarch

½ cup (1 stick) unsalted butter

BATTER

1½ cups sugar

1½ cups Atkinson's biscuit mix with butter flakes

¾ cup milk

To make the topping, place the strawberries, water, and sugar in a large saucepan and cook over medium heat for about 20 minutes, or until the strawberries are soft and tender.

While the strawberry mixture is cooking, combine the water and cornstarch in a jar, then shake the ingredients. When the fruit is cooked, add the cornstarch mixture to the saucepan a little at a time, stirring before adding more. It should reach the consistency of canned pie filling. Remove from the heat and let cool.

Once the fruit topping is cool, preheat the oven to 325°F. Place a 9 by 11-inch pan with a stick of butter in the oven while it is preheating to melt the butter and warm the pan.

To make the batter, combine the sugar and the biscuit mix in a large bowl. Add the milk until the batter reaches the consistency of pancake batter.

Remove the pan with the melted butter from the oven. Pour the batter in the pan, then add the topping, evenly distributing it on top of the batter.

Bake for 40 to 60 minutes, until it reaches an internal temperature of 180°F to 190°F. The crust should be dark brown, but not burned.

Let the cobbler cool slightly before serving with ice cream.

YIELD: 8 to 10 servings

GRILLED DONUT S'MORES
CHRISTINE GOLIC

This dessert is so simple to make but so delicious. It combines two great desserts into one: warm glazed donuts and gooey s'mores. A sure favorite at your next cookout!

Canola oil, for oiling the grill

4 large glazed donuts

4 tablespoons milk chocolate–hazelnut spread, divided

2 cups marshmallow fluff, divided

½ cup graham cracker crumbs divided

½ cup confectioners' sugar

Preheat a grill to high and lightly oil the grill grates with canola oil.

Place the glazed donuts on the grill and cook for 40 seconds on each side to develop grill marks.

Remove the donuts from the grill and carefully slice them in half horizontally using a serrated knife.

Spread ½ cup chocolate-hazelnut spread over the cut side of each of the bottom donuts. Spread ½ cup marshmallow fluff over the cut side of each top donut. Sprinkle 2 tablespoons of the graham cracker crumbs over the marshmallow fluff of the 4 donut halves.

Place the top and bottom donuts together to form a sandwich. Dust the donuts with confectioners' sugar and serve.

YIELD: 4 servings

CARROT CAKE

MARK LAMBERT

This carrot cake has a secret ingredient that helps keep it so moist: a buttermilk glaze! This glaze gets poured onto the three layers of this cake as soon as they come out of the oven. By letting the glaze soak in before putting the frosting on, you ensure a rich and moist cake for all to enjoy.

CAKE

2 cups all-purpose flour

2 teaspoons baking soda

½ teaspoon salt

2 teaspoons ground cinnamon

3 large eggs

2 cups granulated sugar

¾ cup vegetable oil

¾ cup buttermilk

2 teaspoons vanilla extract

2 cups grated carrot

1 (8-ounce) can crushed pineapple, undrained

¼ cup unsweetened coconut flakes

1 cup walnuts, coarsely chopped

BUTTERMILK GLAZE

1 cup sugar

1½ teaspoons baking soda

½ cup buttermilk

1 teaspoon vanilla extract

FROSTING

¾ cup (1½ sticks) unsalted butter

12 ounces cream cheese, softened

3 cups confectioners' sugar

1½ teaspoons vanilla

1 cup chopped walnuts or toasted coconut, for topping (optional)

Preheat the oven to 350°F with a rack in the middle position.

Grease and lightly dust with flour three (8-inch) cake pans. Line each cake pan with a circle of parchment paper so that the cakes are easy to remove.

To make the cake, place the flour, baking soda, salt, and cinnamon in a small bowl and combine. Set aside.

In a separate large bowl, beat the eggs. Then stir in the sugar, vegetable oil, buttermilk, and vanilla. Slowly add the flour mixture to the egg mixture. Beat until smooth.

Fold in the carrots, pineapple, coconut, and walnuts.

Pour the batter into the three pans evenly and place them in the oven on the middle rack.

While the cakes are baking, make the glaze. In a saucepan, bring the sugar, baking soda, and buttermilk to a boil over medium-high heat. Remove from the heat, then stir in the vanilla.

Test the cakes for doneness after 25 to 30 minutes in a convection oven, or 30 to 40 minutes in a conventional oven. They should bounce back when touched or poked. Remove the cakes from the oven and immediately pour ⅓ of the glaze over each cake. Let them sit and cool in the pan for about 15 minutes.

While the cakes are cooling, make the frosting. Add all the frosting ingredients to a large bowl and beat, using an electric mixer, until smooth.

After 15 minutes cooling, the cakes are ready to be frosted. Flip the first cake on a cake plate and remove the parchment paper from the bottom. Cover the layer with frosting, then place a second layer on top and repeat. Add the third cake layer and completely cover the sides with frosting.

Add nuts or toasted coconut, if using, to the outside of the finished cake. Cover and refrigerate for a few hours before serving.

YIELD: 8 servings

CAKE IN A CAN
BRYAN MROCZKA

Instead of using a cupcake tin, use a can! You create individual serving sizes super easily with a fun presentation. The best part about this recipe is you can truly make it your own. Use any flavor cake mix you like and feel free to mix up the frosting combinations!

2 (15.5-ounce) tin cans, emptied and cleaned

Cooking spray, for coating the cans

CAKE
½ (15.25-ounce) box yellow cake mix

½ cup water

¼ cup (½ stick) unsalted butter, melted

1 large egg

¼ teaspoon vanilla extract

FROSTING
2 tablespoons unsalted butter, softened

1 teaspoon vanilla extract

1 tablespoon milk

1½ cups confectioners' sugar

2 maraschino cherries, for garnish

Preheat your oven or grill to 350°F. Spray the inside of the cans with cooking spray. (Fruit filling cans are better to use because they are a bit bigger than vegetable cans.)

To make the cake, place the cake mix, water, butter, egg, and vanilla in a medium bowl and use a mixer set on medium to combine. Fill each can half full with cake batter. Place the cans on a medium cookie sheet.

Bake in the oven or on the grill for 30 to 40 minutes, until an inserted toothpick into the cake comes out clean. Transfer the cans to a cooling rack.

To make the frosting, mix the butter, vanilla, and milk in a medium bowl until smooth. Add the confectioners' sugar, ½ cup at a time, until the frosting has reached the desired consistency.

Run a sharp knife around the inside of each can. Remove the cakes from the cans and frost each one. Garnish with cherries if desired.

YIELD: 2 servings

GRILLED POUND CAKE
with FRESH GRILLED PEACHES
JOHNNY IMBRIOLO

This recipe is the perfect end to a great barbecue, and it can be easily multiplied for a crowd. Grilling the peaches and the pound cake takes no time at all, and you can be sure to wow your guests with your grilling skills!

1 tablespoon granulated sugar

1 tablespoon unsalted butter, melted

½ ripe peach, pit removed

1 (½-inch) slice pound cake

¼ cup fresh whipped cream

1 tablespoon clover honey

1 sprig mint, for garnish

Preheat a grill to medium heat, about 325°F.

Place the sugar and butter in a small bowl and mix until the sugar is dissolved.

Place the peach, cut side down, on the grill and baste with the butter-sugar mixture. Continue to rotate the peach until grill marks form. Cook the peach for about 2 minutes on each side, basting the whole time with the butter and sugar.

Place a slice of pound cake on the grill for about 1 minute on each side, or until lightly browned. Remove the pound cake and place on the center of a plate. Add ¼ of the whipped cream in the center of the pound cake to create a high mound.

Remove the peach from the grill and place on top of the pound cake, leaning up against the whipped cream. Drizzle with honey, garnish with mint, and serve.

YIELD: 1 serving

© James Edward Bates

Chapter 9

DRINKS

PASSION FRUIT and CHARRED JALAPEÑO MEZQUILA

GUY FIERI

This drink that perfectly balances the spice from jalapeño and the tartness from passion fruit is sure to impress any party. Its richness in smoky-sweet flavors is sure to enrich your taste palate, and it is a perfect complement to any meal!

CHARRED JALAPEÑO SYRUP

3 jalapeños

1 cup sugar

1 cup water

DRINK

1 tablespoon kosher salt

2 ounces Santo Mezquila

¾ ounce Cointreau

½ ounce freshly squeezed lime juice

1 ounce passion fruit juice

1 lime wheel, for garnish

To make the charred jalapeño syrup, heat a medium cast-iron skillet over medium-high heat. Once the pan is hot, place the jalapeños in the skillet. Rotate occasionally to char and blister them on all sides, about 3 minutes. Once charred on all sides, remove them from the skillet and let cool.

Cut 2 charred peppers into slices. Reserve the third for garnish.

In a medium saucepan, combine the sugar, water, and jalapeño slices over medium-high heat and bring to a boil. Stir until the sugar is dissolved. Decrease the heat and let simmer for about 3 minutes. Remove the saucepan from the heat and let the liquid steep for 15 to 20 minutes. Remove the jalapeños, pour the liquid into a squeeze bottle, and store it in the refrigerator. It will keep for up to 7 days.

To make the drink, rim a 16-ounce glass with salt, fill it with ice, and set it aside.

Fill a mixing glass ⅔ full with ice and add the Mezquila, Cointreau, lime juice, passion fruit juice, and 1 teaspoon jalapeño syrup. Cap the mixing glass with a shaker tin and shake vigorously for 10 to 15 seconds.

Strain the contents from the shaker tin into the prepared glass. Garnish with a lime wheel and charred jalapeño.

YIELD: 1 serving

LIQUID SMOKE and SMOKED SIMPLE SYRUP

STAN HAYS

This is a unique way to add a subtle hint of smoke to any cocktail. It is best to use large cubes or blocks of ice in a smoker to make your own liquid smoke. Just having a pan of water will only smoke the top of the water. With ice, as it melts, there is more surface area, so more smoke will be absorbed, making your own liquid smoke. You can add the liquid smoke directly to a cocktail or use it to make a sweeter smoked simple syrup.

8-pound block of ice

2 cups sugar, if making simple syrup

Start a smoker and set the temperature low, around 175°F. Add your preferred type of wood to the smoker. Experiment with different types of wood to create different flavor profiles. Place the block of ice in a pan large enough to accommodate the amount of liquid when it melts. Add the pan of ice to the smoker.

Let the ice smoke for about 1½ hours. Remove the pan from the smoker and let it cool.

From here, there are two options: pour the cooled liquid smoke into ice molds or ice cube trays, or take 2 cups of the liquid smoke to make a smoked simple syrup.

To make a simple syrup, combine 2 cups of the liquid smoke and the sugar in a small saucepan. Heat over medium heat on the stovetop to dissolve the sugar, stirring regularly.

Let cool and refrigerate in a covered container. It will keep up to 1 month.

YIELD: 10 to 12 cups liquid

SMOKED CHERRY OLD-FASHIONED

STAN HAYS

A new take on a classic drink. The warmth and spice from bourbon combined with the sweetness of cherries produces this delicious smoky-savory drink with an appealing presentation. By taking the time to smoke the water using cherrywood for a smoked simple syrup, the old-fashioned takes on a new flavor palate.

4 ounces bourbon

2 tablespoons Smoked Simple Syrup (page 146)

4 to 5 dashes Angostura bitters

1 to 2 cubes ice

2 cubes Smoked Cherrywood Ice (page 146)

2 orange twists

Maraschino cherries, for garnish

Place the bourbon, simple syrup, and bitters in a 16-ounce mixing glass or shaker. Add a cube or two of regular ice and stir until well combined.

Strain and divide the mixture into two rocks glasses with one large cherrywood-smoked ice cube each.

Twist the orange peel over the top of each glass, then rub it around the rim, and finally add it to the glass. Stir, garnish with a maraschino cherry, and enjoy.

YIELD: 2 servings

CHARGRILLED PINEAPPLE PIÑA COLADA

MIKE GOLIC

Piña coladas are a sure hit at any party. Kick up your drink a few notches and enhance the flavor of your drink by adding the grilled pineapple. You can show off your grilling skills with a few charred pieces for a garnish!

1 whole pineapple, peeled and cut into 1-inch-wide spears

2 jalapeños, halved and seeded

Cooking spray

4 ounces spiced dark rum

4 ounces unsweetened coconut cream

2 cups ice cubes

Lime wedges, for garnish

Heat a grill to 475°F.

Lightly coat the pineapple and jalapeños with cooking spray and place on the grill for about 1 minute on each side, or until there are grill marks and some char.

Remove the pineapple and jalapeños from the grill and let cool. Then cut the pineapple into cubes and dice the jalapeños. Reserve 4 cubes of charred pineapple in the refrigerator for garnish. Store the charred jalapeño in an airtight container overnight.

Place the pineapple chunks in a resealable plastic bag and freeze them for several hours or overnight.

Combine the pineapple, jalapeños, rum, coconut cream, and ice cubes in a blender. Process on high until smooth.

Pour into your favorite glasses and garnish each with a lime wedge and pineapple cube.

YIELD: 4 servings

CHARGRILLED JALAPEÑO and SMOKED LIME MARGARITA

STAN HAYS

Take your margarita to the next level by using your grill. Combine grilled limes and jalapeños with a smoked simple syrup to make a citrusy, smoky, and super refreshing margarita fit for any barbecue.

10 limes

1 tablespoon margarita salt or sugar in the raw, for glass rimming

1 large jalapeño, halved lengthwise and seeded

1 cup Smoked Simple Syrup (page 146)

1 cup triple sec

1 cup lemon-lime soda

1 cup tequila

1 bottle Corona beer or your favorite Mexican beer

Using a rasp grater, zest one lime. Combine the zest with salt or sugar on a small plate to rim all of the glasses. Set the glasses aside.

Prepare a grill at 325°F.

Cut 9 of the limes (including the zested lime) in half, then cut the tenth into ¼-inch-thick rounds. Grill the lime halves, lime rounds, and jalapeños for about 1½ minutes, or until you start seeing some grill marks. Remove them from the grill to let cool.

Juice the 18 lime halves into a pitcher, trying to keep the seeds out.

Warm the simple syrup with half of the jalapeño in a small saucepan over medium heat on the stovetop. Let it steep in the hot simple syrup for 15 minutes, then remove the jalapeño from the syrup. Let the syrup cool slightly. Add the simple syrup to your mixing pitcher.

Add the triple sec, soda, tequila, and beer. Stir to combine the ingredients well.

Run the lime rounds around each serving glass, a cooler glass or a mason jar, and salt the rim with the lime-zested salt. Julienne the other jalapeño half into thin strips and add a couple strips to each glass.

Fill the prepared glasses full of ice, pour the margarita over the ice, and enjoy!

YIELD: 4 servings

GRILLED STRAWBERRY LEMONADE

MIKE GOLIC

This is a refreshing twist on a favorite backyard beverage. The sweetness of the strawberries is accented with the flavor of the fresh lemonade. This is the perfect drink to serve as a "mocktail" or for kids to enjoy!

12 large lemons

1 pound fresh strawberries, stemmed and halved

½ cup sugar

1 cup agave syrup

2 cups water

Ice

Preheat a grill to 325°F.

Cut the lemons in half and squeeze the juice into a medium bowl.

Place the strawberries and sugar in a large bowl and gently toss.

Place the strawberries on the heated grill, cut side down, and grill for 30 seconds. Remove the strawberries from the grill and allow them to cool.

Place the lemon juice, agave syrup, and water in a blender.

Place half of the grilled strawberries in the blender. Pulse the blender to chop the strawberries. Do not overblend.

Pour the lemonade into a pitcher and add the remaining grilled strawberries. Top with fresh ice and serve.

YIELD: 2 servings

Chapter 10
RUBS AND SAUCES

CHIPOTLE BUTTER

Compound butters are designed to add depth of flavor to any dish you are preparing. This recipe combines the subtle smoky flavor of the chipotle pepper with just a touch of sweet citrus. Chipotle Butter is a key ingredient in Chipotle-Smoked Chicken (page 77).

1 pound (4 sticks) unsalted butter, at room temperature

10 tablespoons chipotle peppers in adobo sauce

6 tablespoons light brown sugar

6 tablespoons freshly squeezed lime juice

1½ teaspoons kosher salt

Place the butter in a food processor and blend. Add the remaining ingredients and blend until all the ingredients are well mixed.

Spoon the butter mixture onto a piece of plastic wrap and roll so the butter forms one log that is 1½ inches in diameter.

Place in the refrigerator. This will keep for 1 week.

YIELD: 1 pound

RYDERDIE SEASONING
MIKE RAMSEY AND JIM FURYK

Chef Mike Ramsey attended the Ryder Cup with professional golfer Jim Furyk, and he served as their team chef during the tournament. While in Paris for the Ryder Cup, Chef Ramsey showed other players and teams the ways of the American barbecue! This seasoning is inspired by Jim Furyk and their time together golfing and eating delicious food. This is a great all-purpose seasoning for pork, chicken, and beef. One key element of this seasoning is its lack of salt, which makes it very versatile.

½ cup sweet paprika

½ cup smoked paprika

½ cup coarse-ground black pepper

1 cup turbinado sugar

¼ cup Korean chili powder

1 tablespoon cayenne pepper

2 tablespoons ground mustard

2 tablespoons ground cumin

2 tablespoons soy sauce powder

2 tablespoons porcini powder

2 tablespoons ground white pepper

Place all the ingredients in a medium bowl and use a whisk to blend together (or place all the ingredients in a food processor to combine).

To use as a barbecue rub, season a meat of choice with kosher salt first, then apply the rub liberally.

To use as an all-purpose seasoning, add 1 tablespoon kosher salt to 1 cup seasoning.

Store in an airtight container for up to 6 weeks.

YIELD: 3½ cups

KANSAS CITY STEAK SEASONING

This is a robust seasoning that is fantastic on steak but can also be used on chicken and pork. You can use this rub as you prepare the Prime Rib with Horseradish Sauce (page 70) or any night of the week you are making steaks on the grill.

2 tablespoons black peppercorns

2 teaspoons mustard seeds

1 tablespoon smoked paprika

1 tablespoon coarse salt

1 tablespoon dried or garlic powder

1 tablespoon red pepper flakes

1 tablespoon dried or onion powder

1 tablespoon light brown sugar

1 teaspoon chile powder

Place the peppercorns and mustard seeds in a resealable plastic bag, release the air, and seal. Roll a rolling pin over the peppercorns and mustard seeds to crush them to a coarse grind. Place in a small bowl. Add the remaining ingredients and mix well.

Store in a sealed, airtight container for up to 8 weeks.

YIELD: About 5 ounces

SOUTHWEST FAJITA RUB

Looking for a great way to add a pop of flavor to your grilled items? Look no further—this rub is great on beef, chicken, pork, and even vegetables! Any night you want to have Mexican-style food, throw this seasoning on your meat. You will be able to whip up tacos or fajitas with bold Southwest flavors using this rub!

1 tablespoon chili powder

1 tablespoon ground cumin

2 teaspoons garlic powder

1 teaspoon onion powder

1 teaspoon smoked paprika

1 teaspoon kosher salt

½ teaspoon ground chipotle pepper

1 teaspoon dried oregano

Place all the ingredients in a small bowl and whisk until completely blended.

Store in an airtight container or resealable plastic bag for up to 6 weeks.

YIELD: ¼ cup

CITRUS RUB

This rub is specifically designed for poultry and seafood, but it can also be used for pork. The subtle citrus flavors combined with Latin-style undertones will jazz up anything you are grilling. Use this rub as you prepare the Mojo-Marinated Chicken Skewers (page 80) or any of the salmon dishes found in the cookbook.

1 tablespoon dry orange peel

1 tablespoon dry lemon peel

2 tablespoons kosher salt

2 tablespoons light brown sugar

2 tablespoons ground cumin

1 teaspoon smoked paprika

1 teaspoon ground white pepper

1 teaspoon dried cilantro

1 teaspoon onion powder

1 teaspoon garlic powder

Place the lemon peel and orange peel in a small, clean grinder and blend until they reach a fine grind. Add to a medium bowl.

Add the remaining ingredients to the bowl and mix well. Store in an airtight container for up to 6 weeks.

YIELD: About 5 ounces

SALT, PEPPER, and GARLIC RUB

This rub is a base seasoning that can be used on EVERYTHING! From steak to chicken to vegetables, you can't go wrong with this rub. It's a simple blend of—you guessed it—salt, pepper, and garlic, which allows it to be very versatile. Add this to meats, mac 'n' cheese, vegetables—anything you think needs some extra flavor!

½ cup kosher salt

½ cup slightly coarse-ground black pepper

¼ cup garlic powder

Place all the ingredients in a small bowl and mix. Store in an airtight container for up to 6 weeks.

YIELD: 1¼ cups

TEXAS BRISKET RUB

Smoking brisket in Texas is a mainstay. Texans take great pride in their brisket, and this rub is one of the best from the Lone Star State. You can use this rub as you prepare your brisket for the Southwest Brisket Chili (page 60) or for the brisket in the Brisket-Stuffed Jalapeños (page 2).

1 tablespoon kosher salt

2 tablespoons garlic powder

2 tablespoons onion powder

4 tablespoons smoked paprika

1 teaspoon cayenne pepper

2 tablespoons light brown sugar

2 tablespoons sugar

2 tablespoons ground cumin

Place all the ingredients in a small bowl and mix until the rub is well blended.

Store in an airtight container for up to 8 weeks.

YIELD: 1 cup

CAROLINA–STYLE VINEGAR BARBECUE MOP

This is the perfect barbecue mop, from pork butts to half chicken to whole hog. This mop is done in the traditional Carolina style, meaning it utilizes lots of vinegar in its preparation. A mop differs from a sauce because it is much thinner and waterier. It is applied using a barbecue mop and helps prevent meats from drying out over an open flame.

1½ cups distilled white vinegar

4 ounces ketchup

6 ounces hot sauce

3 tablespoons crushed red pepper

Place all the ingredients in a large bowl and whisk to combine.

Use as a mop on desired meats. Refrigerate in an airtight container for up to 1 week.

YIELD: 3 cups

HOMEMADE BARBECUE SAUCE

This barbecue sauce is super easy to make. It has just the right amount of sweet, heat, and vinegar to complement anything you're cooking on your grill. This sauce would work well on the Barbecue Pulled Pork Flatbread (page 51) or on the Smoked Barbecue Reuben (page 99).

1½ cups ketchup

1 cup firmly packed light brown sugar

½ cup water

¼ cup apple cider vinegar

1 tablespoon Worcestershire sauce

1 tablespoon molasses

1 teaspoon kosher salt

½ teaspoon garlic powder

½ teaspoon onion powder

¼ teaspoon yellow mustard

¼ teaspoon smoked paprika

¼ teaspoon hot sauce

¼ teaspoon ground cumin

Place all the ingredients in a large saucepot over high heat. Mix well until all the ingredients are incorporated and bring to a boil.

Once the sauce starts to boil, decrease the heat to a simmer. Simmer for about 20 minutes. Remove it from the heat and allow to cool. Store in an airtight container in the refrigerator for up to 1 week.

YIELD: 2½ cups

SWEET 'N' SASSY BARBECUE SAUCE

This balanced barbecue sauce is the perfect sauce to add to your chicken, ribs, or pulled pork—just enough sweet to add that last layer of flavor to whatever you are cooking. Use this barbecue sauce as you prepare the Sweet 'n' Sassy Barbecue Spatchcocked Chicken (page 82).

2 cups firmly packed light brown
   sugar

1½ cups ketchup

½ cup honey

½ cup red wine vinegar

½ cup apple cider vinegar

1 tablespoon Worcestershire sauce

2½ tablespoons dry mustard

2 teaspoons smoked paprika

2 teaspoons kosher salt

1½ teaspoons black pepper

Place all the ingredients in a medium saucepan over medium heat and whisk until smooth. Cook for 20 minutes. Refrigerate in an airtight container for up to 1 week.

YIELD: 3 cups

BARBECUE MUSTARD SAUCE

This is a great barbecue sauce for those who really enjoy mustard and spice. It is great on pulled pork or even ribs. Using this sauce with the Smoked Pork Loin Sandwich (page 98) will add some extra kick and tangy flavor to the meal.

½ cup apple cider vinegar

3 tablespoons barbecue sauce

2 tablespoons chipotle peppers in adobo sauce

1 cup yellow mustard

¼ cup clover honey

¼ cup firmly packed light brown sugar

1 teaspoon garlic powder

Place the vinegar, barbecue sauce, and chipotle peppers in a food processor and blend until smooth.

Transfer the mixture to a medium saucepan and add the mustard, honey, brown sugar, and garlic.

Stir well and place over medium heat, stirring often. When the sauce begins to boil, remove the pan from the heat. The temperature of the sauce must reach 165°F.

Serve immediately. This sauce can be refrigerated in an airtight container for up to 1 week.

YIELD: 3 cups

Chef Biographies

Matt Besler is a defender on the Austin FC team in Major League Soccer (MLS). Besler previously played for Sporting Kansas City, where he helped them win an MLS Cup. In addition to Besler's hard work on the field, he is a dedicated servant in his community. He partnered with the Leukemia and Lymphoma Society for the Man of the Year campaign and was named W.O.R.K.S. Humanitarian of the Month by MLS.

Rocky Bleier is a former NFL halfback for the Pittsburgh Steelers, where he was a part of four Super Bowl victories. He played in the NFL after graduating from the University of Notre Dame. In addition to his football career, Bleier also served in the US Army during the Vietnam War. Since leaving the NFL, he has become an author, public speaker, and radio show host.

Ben Braunecker played college football at Harvard and was signed by the Chicago Bears. He played tight end for the Bears for four years.

Reggie Brooks is a former NFL running back who played in the NFL for three years for the Washington Football Team and the Tampa Bay Buccaneers. He played college football at the University of Notre Dame and earned All-American honors. Brooks later went on to serve as the assistant athletics director, athletic alumni relations, at the university, where he works closely with student-athletes and student-athlete alumni. Brooks now serves as the executive director of the Holtz's Heroes Foundation, a charitable organization founded by famed football coach Lou Holtz.

Tom Burgmeier is a former Major League Baseball relief pitcher who played for the California Angels, Kansas City Royals, Minnesota Twins, Boston Red Sox, and Oakland A's.

Clarence Ceasar was roommates with Shaquille O'Neal during his time at Louisiana State University. Now Ceasar works closely with the local government in Lake Charles, Louisiana. Operation BBQ Relief has worked with residents in Lake Charles on two deployments and served over 400,000 meals to the community after hurricanes in 2020.

Mark Collins was drafted by the New York Giants in the second round of the 1986 NFL Draft after playing at Cal State-Fullerton. Mark also played for the Kansas City Chiefs, the Green Bay Packers, and the Seattle Seahawks. While with the Giants, Mark was a two-time Super Bowl Champion. Mark's passion and mission is to help student athletes across the country further their education at the collegiate level while excelling in the sport they love playing.

Dewayne Daniel is the Operation BBQ Relief director of disaster coordination, and he competes on the Memphis BBQ Network with the Rack Pack out of Jonesboro, Arkansas. The Rack Pack finished in the top three in the rib division at Memphis in May 2011 and 2014. Daniel also competes in KCBS with the RedNeck Grillers out of Kennett, Missouri, where they have collected 24 Grand Championships and numerous Reserve Grands. They had a first-place finish at the American Royal Open in the brisket category in 2011. Daniel and the We Are OBR team won the Houston Livestock Show and Rodeo World BBQ Championship in 2019.

Guy Fieri is one of the most recognizable chefs in America, as he owns multiple restaurants, hosts famous television shows on the Food Network, and publishes several of his own cookbooks. Fieri loves educating others about food, and he is a great supporter of law enforcement and the military. His relationship with Operation BBQ Relief started when he called the organization to come help

last 20 years. He identifies as a Southern chef, but he also creatively reinterprets classic Southern fare by incorporating the refinement of his French culinary training, along with his signature bold flavors and the occasional flair from his family's Jamaican recipes.

Kyle Rudolph is a current NFL tight end who was drafted in 2011 to the Minnesota Vikings. In 2021, he signed to play for the New York Giants. He has been selected to two Pro Bowls. Before his NFL career, Rudolph played football at the University of Notre Dame. He and his wife, Jordan, are passionate about serving the communities in which he plays.

Carl Ruiz was a chef known for his modern takes on Cuban cuisine. He starred in various Food Network shows such as *Guy's Grocery Games* and *Diners, Drive-Ins, and Dives*. Ruiz also opened his own restaurant called La Cubana, as a nod to his Cuban heritage.

For over 25 years, Chef **Kathy Ruiz** has served as an exceptional leader as the senior vice president of culinary for Fertitta Entertainment. Ruiz's outstanding talent has contributed greatly to the success of some of Landry's most notable restaurants and hotels, including Mastro's Steakhouse, Morton's the Steakhouse, Chart House, Del Frisco's, the five iconic Golden Nugget Casinos and Resorts, and Houston's *Forbes* five-star award-winning hotel, the Post Oak Hotel at Uptown Houston. In addition to overseeing menu preparation, Ruiz organizes the culinary program for the NBA's Houston Rockets. Prior to joining Landry's, Ruiz owned and operated her restaurant, Kathy's, specializing in farm-to-table cuisine.

Bret Saberhagen's notable Major League Baseball career spanned 18 years. He led the Kansas City Royals to their first World Series Championship in 1985, where he was named MVP of the series. He has been awarded two Cy

Young Awards and a Gold Glove, has been inducted into the Royals Hall of Fame, and is a three-time All-Star. While baseball was Saberhagen's passion early in life, his passions have evolved to include giving back to others. His work includes mentoring addicts and working with the youth to teach them the positive effects of devoting time to their communities and those in need.

Kandace Saberhagen, Bret's wife, is the former president and business strategist directly responsible for providing leadership and development for several companies. She is an avid public speaker and author. She also advocates for cancer patients while sharing her personal experiences as a three-time breast cancer survivor. Bret and Kandace have created the nonprofit SabesWings. Its mission is to strike out medical financial toxicity for individuals suffering from cancer. Together, they are building a strong foundation of support for others dealing with insurmountable circumstances.

Mitch Schwartz is a Super Bowl Champion NFL offensive tackle who played for he Cleveland Browns and the Kansas City Chiefs. Schwartz has been a key supporter of the mission of Operation BBQ Relief. He featured Operation BBQ Relief during the NFL's My Cause, My Cleats programs.

Aarti Sequeira is an Indian-American cook who was the Food Network's winner of the sixth season of *The Next Food Network Star*. After her win, she went on to host her own show on the Food Network called *Aarti Party*. She is best known for taking traditional American dishes and adding Indian influences to them. Sequeria credits most of her culinary inspiration to her Indian background and, specifically, her mother's influence.

Joey Smith is based out of San Antonio, Texas, and has been competing for 15 years. Smith and his team have a combined 80-plus Grand Champions and Reserve Grand

Champions and one World Championship. Smith recently started his own barbecue spice and sauce business in 2019. He loves barbecue and the fans and family who come along with it.

Art Still is a former defensive end for the NFL, where he played for the Buffalo Bills and the Kansas City Chiefs. He played in the NFL for 11 years and was named to the Kansas City Chiefs Hall of Fame in 1998. Art serves as a board member for Operation BBQ Relief.

Chef **Michael Symon** hails from Cleveland, Ohio, from a family of Mediterranean and Eastern European descent, which greatly influences how he cooks. In Cleveland, he owns Lola, Mabel's BBQ, Roast, Bar Symon, Angeline, and B Spot Burgers. Symon also showcases his cooking talents on *Iron Chef* on the Food Network, and he served as a former cohost on ABC's *The Chew*.

Chef **Jet Tila** is internationally celebrated for his culinary expertise, from battling on Iron Chef America and opening Encore hotel in Las Vegas to guiding Anthony Bourdain through many markets and restaurants around the world. This Emmy and James Beard nominee and bestselling author grew up in the first family of Thai food and then later attended both French and Japanese culinary schools. Tila was appointed as the inaugural Culinary Ambassador of Thai Cuisine by the Royal Thai Consulate, the first-ever chef to represent his country's culture and cuisine. He appears as cohost of *Iron Chef America* and a recurring judge on Food Network's *Cutthroat Kitchen*, *Chopped*, *Beat Bobby Flay*, and *Guy's Grocery Games*, and he holds six culinary Guinness World Records.

Kurt Warner is a man who continually beat the odds as quarterback to lead two different franchises to the Super Bowl and etched his name in the NFL record books. **Brenda Warner** is a former marine, a registered nurse, and

a gifted speaker. Kurt's gridiron accomplishments pale in comparison to the dedication he and Brenda devote to the community. In 2001, they established the First Things First Foundation, a nonprofit public charity dedicated to impacting lives by promoting Christian values, sharing experiences, and providing opportunities to encourage everyone that all things are possible when people seek to put *first things first*. In 2012, Kurt and Brenda founded Treasure House (www.treasurehouse.org), a residential facility for young adults with intellectual and developmental disabilities. Kurt and Brenda live in Arizona and have seven children and two grandchildren.

Trey Wingo is a former NFL Studio host, SportsCenter anchor, and cohost of ESPN radio show *Golic & Wingo*. Wingo started his 23-year ESPN career as a play-by-play announcer for the Arena Football League. He then went on to host *NFL Primetime* as well. Outside of work, Wingo is involved with various charity organizations, including serving as an official supporter of the Ronald McDonald House Charities.

Nick Woolfolk currently serves as manager of culinary operations at Operation BBQ Relief. At age 10, he began joining his father at local barbecue contests with his friends to enjoy the festivities, but something caught Woolfolk's eye that changed him forever: barbecue. By age 14, he was traveling with the legendary Natural Born Grillers as their rib cook and also sharing his young knowledge with teams on the circuit. While in college, Woolfolk began cooking full time while volunteering with Operation BBQ Relief as a pitmaster who specialized in large mass feedings. In 2019, he took the position of head pitmaster with Operation BBQ Relief. Finally, he took a position as pitmaster for the acclaimed Pig Beach BBQ out of Brooklyn, New York, joining them in opening their new southern outpost in Palm Beach, Florida.

Acknowledgments

We extend our gratitude to volunteers, sponsors, and supporters that further the mission of Operation BBQ Relief since we began in 2011. We are grateful to the editorial and design team from Andrews McMeel Publishing with special thanks to Hugh Andrews, Jean Lucas, and Holly Swayne for believing in our vision for *Grilling with Golic and Hays*. The Andrews and McMeel families have been instrumental in providing scholarships toward the summer service internship program through the University of Notre Dame. Since 2020, seven Andrews Scholars have participated in summer internships with Operation BBQ Relief.

Special thanks to the incredible photography skills of Ken Goodman along with Jeremy Lock, and Mike and Sue Bennett from Lighthouse Imaging. Thank you to the amazing staff whose dedication and expertise in the areas of culinary, operations, programs, legal counsel, human resources, and marketing further the mission of the organization each day. Lastly, we thank the talented chefs, sports celebrities, and pitmasters who are true champions on and off the field and grill and in the kitchen that made this cookbook a reality.

Million Meal Milestones

Operation BBQ Relief takes pride in the number of meals they have served to communities in need since 2011. They have developed their own proprietary software application that tracks meals counts and takes orders from organizations that need meals during deployments and special events. The software allows the organization to be able to run reports, track trending, and gather important data to act quickly and make organizational decisions during and after a deployment.

In 2016, Operation BBQ Relief celebrated the one millionth meal served in Hammond, Louisiana following catastrophic flooding. Over 313, 000 meals were served to Louisiana residents and first responders affected by the flooding. They returned to this same community, many of millions of meals later, in August 2021 to serve 247,055 meals.

Hammond, Louisiana (August 27, 2016)

Wilmington, North Carolina (September 24, 2018)

Bahamas (September 19, 2019)

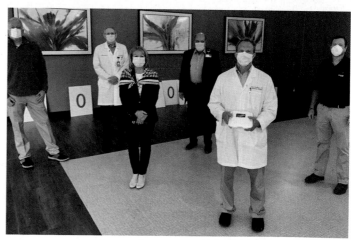

Kansas City, Kansas (May 7, 2020)

Nashville, Tennessee (May 20, 2020)

Los Angeles, California (May 28, 2020)

Reading, Pennsylvania (June 17, 2020)

Cedar Rapids, Iowa (August 21, 2020)

Houston, Texas (February 24, 2021)

"In Febraury 2021, a historic winter storm left many families displaced and unable to prepare meals for their loved ones in the greater Houston area. Without hesitation, Operation BBQ Relief provided hot meals to thousands of Houstonians recovering from freezing weather.

"I was fortunate to team up with the organization to serve the nine millionth meal. It was heartwarming to know that stomachs were full and to see the smiles on the faces of adults and children.

"Operation BBQ Relief has made an extraordinary difference all over the country. I thank them for their work and will be forever grateful for the relief and recovery response they provided in Houston."

—Mayor Sylvester Turner, City of Houston